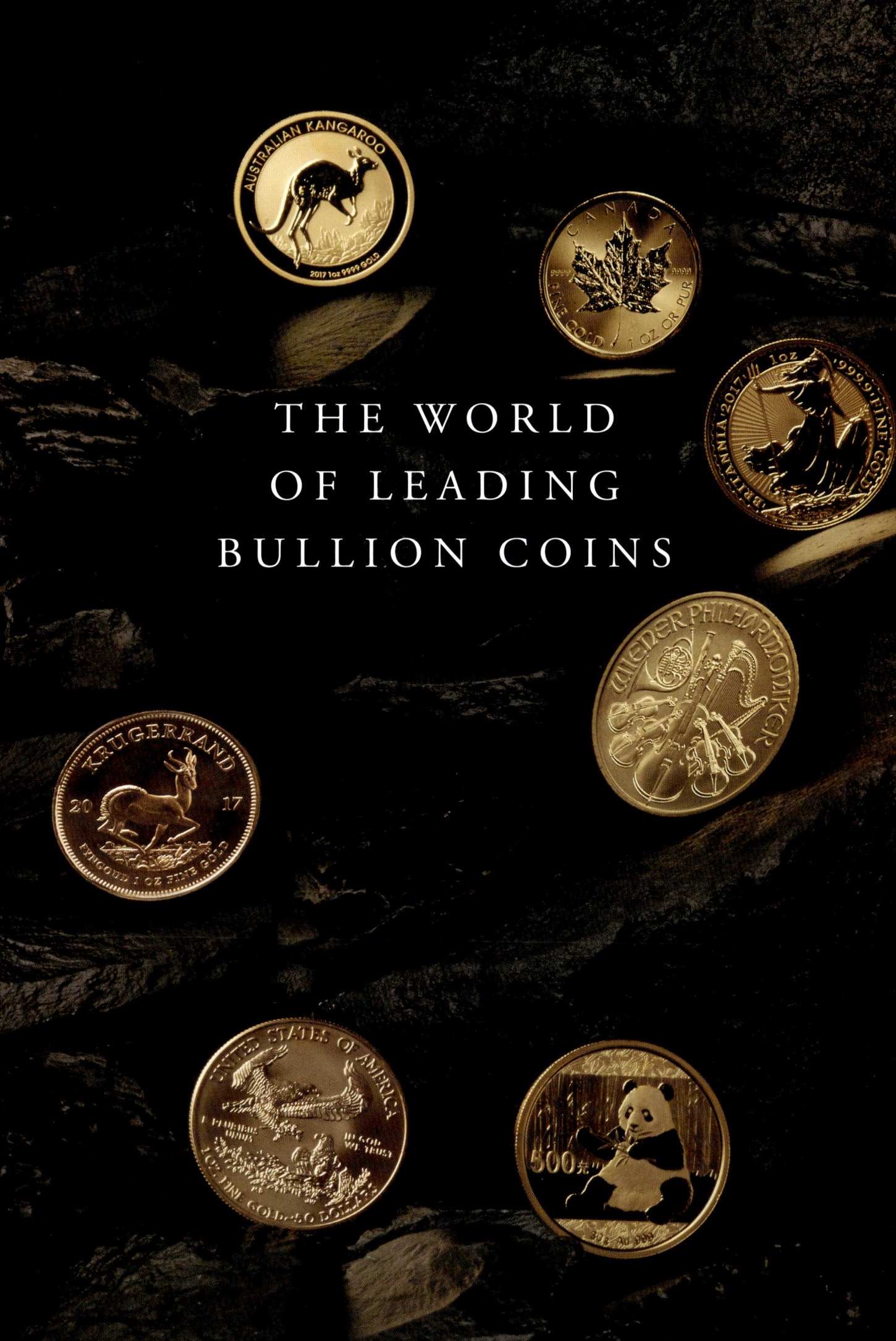

THE WORLD
OF LEADING
BULLION COINS

Design and art direction by Annie Tidyman (tidythinking@gmail.com).
Photography supplied by individual mints, additional shots taken by Lee Kelsey & Latifu Laoye.
We would like to thank Baird & Co. for their support with the photography.

This book was published and printed by Leo Paper Group.
Printed in China.

ISBN (Hardback): 978-0-9935876-9-6
ISBN (Online): 978-1-9997997-0-0

THE WORLD
OF LEADING
BULLION COINS

This book was produced by Metals Focus, the world's leading precious metals consultancy. They specialise in research into the global gold, silver, platinum and palladium markets, producing regular reports, forecasts, proprietary data and bespoke consultancy.

The quality of Metals Focus' work is underpinned by a combination of top-quality desk-based analysis, coupled with an extensive program of travel to generate 'bottom up' research for our forecasting reports and consultancy services. Our analysts regularly travel to the major markets speaking to contacts from across the value chain from producers to consumers.

Contact details:
Unit T, Reliance Wharf, 2-10 Hertford Road, London, N1 5ET
Telephone: +44 20 3301 6510, Email: info@metalsfocus.com
Bloomberg Metals Focus Launch Page: MTFO
Bloomberg chat: IB MFOCUS

www.metalsfocus.com

CONTENTS

FOREWORD

Private ownership of gold coins can be traced back several thousand years. The ancient Lydians (in modern day Turkey) were one of the first civilisations to use gold in coins some 2,700 years ago. The fact that government-minted bullion coins are still relevant to investors and collectors today is testament to the advantages that their ownership can bring as a portable store of value. These include direct exposure to the underlying precious metal value, the integrity of the state owned mints, the legal tender status of many bullion coins and ease with which they can be purchased and readily sold as the need arises. These characteristics help explain the surge in investor demand for bullion coins during and since the last financial crisis, as investors shifted their focus towards precious metals.

The era of the modern bullion coin started with the launch of the 22-carat gold bullion Krugerrand in 1967. During the late 1970s and 1980s the bullion coin sector quickly expanded to include the Canadian Maple Leaf (1979), the Chinese Panda (1982), the American Eagle (1986), the Australian Kangaroo and the UK Britannia (1987) and the Austrian Vienna Philharmonic (1989). It should also be noted that the British Sovereign was re-launched in 1957, in response to the popularity of the South African R1 and R2 gold coins, which were first issued in 1952.

In addition to gold, the development of silver bullion coins has also continued, while the entry of platinum and more recently palladium coins has enabled investors to gain exposure across the precious metal complex. Overall, many of these coins have had a significant bearing on their respective markets. Taken together, modern gold bullion coins have consumed approximately 5,000 tonnes (160 million ounces) of gold, while silver bullion coins have accounted for around 33,000 tonnes (1,060 million ounces) of silver demand.

Against this backdrop, Metals Focus has prepared this reference book, featuring the world's leading newly minted bullion coins, representing the vast majority of those traded in the international market. This book also touches on why gold continues to resonate with the investor community and looks at some of the other ways in which investors can gain exposure to precious metals.

"The World of Leading Bullion Coins" would not have been possible without the generous support and co-sponsorship of The Perth Mint in Australia, The Austrian Mint, The Royal Canadian Mint, The Rand Refinery in South Africa and The Royal Mint in the United Kingdom. We trust this book will add to your understanding of the bullion coin market. Its preparation has certainly been a fascinating journey for the Metals Focus team.

Philip Newman, *Director, Metals Focus*

INVESTING IN GOLD

THE RATIONALE FOR HOLDING GOLD

For centuries gold has been seen by many investors as the ultimate store of value. Historically, its scarcity and indestructibility made it an obvious choice. Meanwhile, in recent times, its zero or even negative correlation with traditional investments, such as equities, has driven many investors looking for a way to diversify their portfolios to the metal.

There are several reasons why holding gold has stood the test of time. We could begin with gold's physical properties, in particular its scarcity, beauty, unique colour, ductility as well as permanence. Its historically high value is also critical.

These characteristics have resulted in gold having had a long history as a medium of exchange. To take just one example, the Venetian gold ducat was accepted as a means of international payments across the Mediterranean in Medieval times. This role has now all but disappeared and so no longer drives the possession of gold coins and bars. However, that is quite separate from gold's more important role, acting as a store of value. This function very much remains relevant and acts as the underlying driver of gold ownership.

This store of value as well as gold's ability to act as a means of wealth preservation is based on a wide range of factors. Among the most important is gold's perceived ability to act as a hedge against inflation. A clear illustration of that can be found in gold in Germany today, as memories of hyperinflation mean that retail investment there is roughly ten times that of the UK. That in turn reflects a crucial difference between gold and paper money; a government can provide an effectively limitless supply of a fiat currency, whereas the supply of gold is constrained by the ability of miners to dig this comparatively rare metal out of the ground.

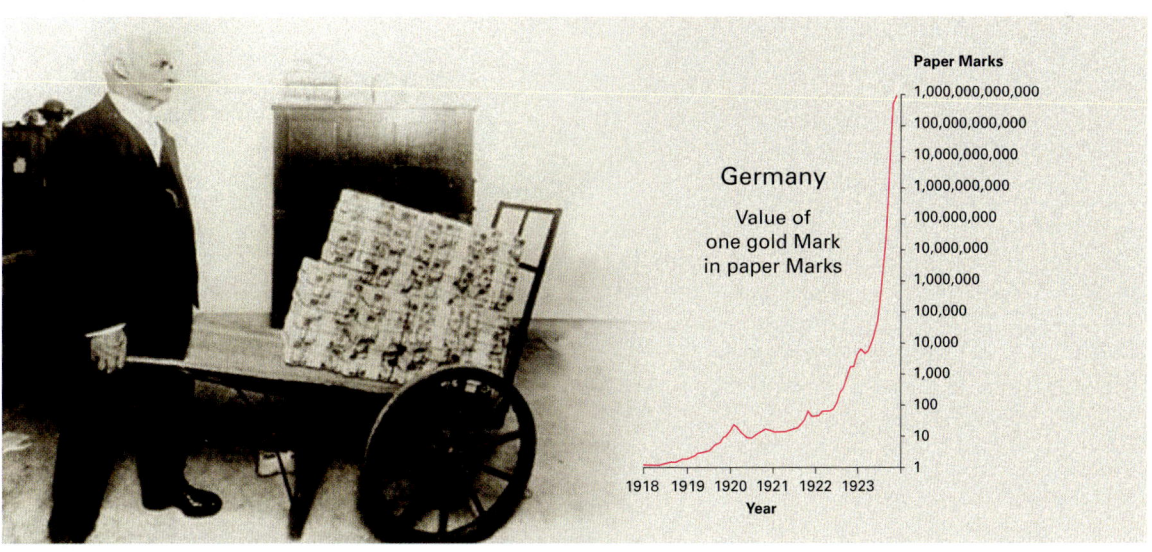

Logarithmic chart of German Hyperinflation. Take from The Economics of Inflation by Costantino Bresciani-Turroni, published 1937.

That gold is not beholden to governments is another key characteristic of the metal, namely that it essentially has no counterparty risk. Many traditional assets, such as bonds or equities, are reliant on the actions of others, governments and corporate management boards in this instance. For example, it was gold's independence that helped explain the wave of investment it saw following the Lehman Brothers' bust in September 2008, when confidence in other assets plummeted.

The tendency of the gold price to have a negative correlation with other assets also helps explain why gold is popular as a portfolio diversifier.

In contrast to all these benefits, investing in gold has a fundamental challenge, in that it generates no yield. That disadvantage fades when real interest rates are low or negative and grows when real interest rates are high. It is this relationship that partly explains the sensitivity of gold prices to changes in interest rates, particularly in the US.

The fact that gold is priced in dollars can also act as a stimulant for investment where governments have capital controls; if an individual cannot readily invest overseas, the purchase of gold locally acts as a proxy acquisition of dollars. That has been a factor for some investors in China recently for example. More generally, individuals in some countries may wish to store their money discretely in gold, for example to avoid reporting requirements.

Cultural factors can also act as a stimulus for investment in gold. A good example is the dowry that a bride receives in India. Traditionally, this is primarily in the form of gold jewellery, but there has been a shift over time towards bars and coins, as these carry a lower margin over the fine metal price. While buyers in India

The Bank of England has one of the world's largest gold vaults. At the end of 2016, the facility contained over 164 million ounces of gold.

may stick to locally produced coins and bars, this will be less true of the Indian diaspora, in such countries as Canada or the UK. Finally, gold can also play the trump card of geography, with the metal readily tradeable in most jurisdictions.

Investment in gold is complimented by the option of acquiring other precious metals. Silver's lower unit value means it enjoys a lower entry price point and this also promoted its greater historic use as a medium of exchange. Over the past decade or so, purchases of silver coins and bars have grown tremendously, especially in the US and India, by far the world's two largest markets for physical silver investment. This is despite relatively high storage and transportation costs (in comparison to the value of the contained silver) and also the fact that silver is often subject to VAT, the case in the European Union for example.

Finally, platinum and palladium have similar physical characteristics to gold and are closer in price. They tend to be popular with investors who prefer these metals' prices being more closely linked to supply/demand fundamentals, rather than financial considerations such as bond yields. Both, however, remain challenged by far lower liquidity in physical markets, which can make buy/sell spreads unattractive.

HOW TO INVEST IN PRECIOUS METALS

The evolution of the precious metals market in recent decades means that investors benefit from several options in which to buy into the market. These include coins and bars, exchange traded products, mining equities, the futures and over-the-counter (OTC) markets and e-gold platforms. A brief overview of some of these options follows.

Looking first at coins and bars, these tend to be popular with retail investors for several reasons. First, there is the low entry price point, given the availability of, for example, fractional coins. Second, investment gold in many locations is tax free, including a number of US states, European Union, Australia, Canada and Singapore and in some cases investing in certain bullion coins is even exempt from capital gains tax (such as the Britannia in the UK).

Third, there is an absence of counterparty risk. Next, portability and the perceived ability to use these products for transactions (should the financial system collapse) makes them attractive to some. Finally, a safe haven motive makes it attractive to take delivery, although this can introduce security concerns or storage costs.

There are numerous products on offer in this market. Starting with bullion coins, these are available in 1oz and fractional sizes for gold, platinum and palladium, while silver (given its low value) is only minted as a 1oz piece. Premiums are lowest for 1oz coins. Purities vary for gold coins, from 91.67% for a Krugerrand, Sovereign and Eagle, up to 99.99% for the Vienna Philharmonic, Maple Leaf, Kangaroo and Panda. Meanwhile, silver coins are struck in 99.9% and 99.99% metal, while PGMs are often issued in a 99.95% fineness. Each of the above bullion coins is minted by a government backed mint.

THE IMPORTANCE OF SECONDARY COIN MARKETS

In addition to the primary coin market, which includes sales of newly minted pieces from the mints to investors, through the network of dealers and distributors, there is also an active secondary market for bullion coins. This generally comprises coins that have been minted in past years and are held by investors, being sold back to dealers and ultimately again to other investors. This is a fundamental component of the bullion coin market and is essential to maintaining liquidity and keeping buy/sell spreads tight.

The existence of such a secondary market also provides investors with the peace of mind that, should they wish to liquidate their bullion coin investments in the future, there is an efficient and transparent mechanism in which to do so. In this regard, bullion coins offer a key advantage, as major mints' reputations and production processes offer a guarantee of purity, weight and providence.

Prices for old coins offered or paid by dealers are a function of the underlying metal price, the availability of and investor appetite for a particular type of coin and year and other factors such as the condition of the pieces being sold back and refining costs. This dynamic relationship to the metal price results in price spreads, both between bid-offer and between newly minted and old coins changing over time.

For example, during times of heavy liquidations, the discount compared to the current asking price for a newly minted coin will tend to deepen. The opposite will tend to happen during periods of heightened coin demand, especially if they result in product shortages.

Differences in premiums of secondary and newly minted coins can also affect investor decisions. Price-conscious buyers will often switch between different brands and between new and old coins, depending on what option will offer them the best price.

Premiums may finally also drive wholesaler and dealer behaviour. One key example of this is when investor appetite differs across countries, fuelling inventory transfers between them. For example, dealers may buy back coins from a country where liquidations are heavy and thus discounts deep and ship them to another location where demand is stronger and they can benefit from a higher premium.

Cortez gold mine in Nevada, USA.

Moving to small bars, a range of minted and cast sizes are available, while weights over 100g tend to be cast. The purity of bars also varies, typically from 99.5% to 99.99%, although there are some regional markets where lower purities are also seen. Overall, the preference for a brand, weight (metric or imperial) or purity varies by market. For example, 10g, 20g and 50g minted pieces are popular in China, compared with 1oz bars in the US. Elsewhere, non-standard weights reflect local traditions, such as the tael bar which is popular in parts of East Asia (traditionally a minimum 99 purity and 37.5g weight). Premiums also vary, with cast bars less expensive than minted. There is also an inverse relationship between weight and premium.

Turning to exchange traded products (ETPs), these are securities that are listed on stock exchanges that provide exposure to precious metals prices. They tend to be fully collateralised and so eliminate counterparty risk. The most popular and liquid precious metals ETPs are backed by physical metal and specifically allocated positions (these are segregated from other holdings and so cannot be leased out). Storage and administrative costs are passed on to investors through fees which vary across metals and products. Finally, ETP owners can often request physical delivery.

ETPs are attractive to some investors as they offer transparency, liquidity and ease of access. As ETP shares tend to be equivalent to a fraction of one ounce, they also offer a cost-effective, low entry threshold to precious metals investments.

However, for some retail investors holding gold as a hedge against a major geopolitical crisis, vault storage and physical delivery limitations can make ETPs seem unattractive. In addition, cost and reporting requirements (and hence their transparency) may be a disadvantage for some large investors.

With regards to mining equities, these offer a popular route to gain exposure to precious metals, as most mining companies are listed on one of the principal stock exchanges. As a result, these equities are easily accessible, generally highly liquid and can generate a yield through dividends. However, investing in mining equities also results in exposure to the mining companies themselves, and the risks associated with operating a mine, not to mention geographical concerns and potential "acts of god". Investors must also appreciate the nature of the company's revenue stream. While precious metals mining companies often focus on one metal, the complex nature of ore deposits mean the primary metal is commonly found with other precious and base metals.

Other key points for investors to consider include an appreciation of the cost structure of a miner's portfolio of mines and projects, not just in absolute terms, but where they sit relative to their peers. The management team's track record can also have a significant bearing on its valuation.

The final options we will consider here are commodity exchanges and OTC trading. The former includes platforms that allow the trading of commodity derivatives. They are commonly centrally cleared, minimising counterparty risk. Futures and options usually commit to physical delivery at a predetermined future date, but they are often settled for cash prior to maturity. Investors will often enter into these contracts with little intention of ever owning the underlying asset, but are simply placing a bet on future prices.

The most liquid precious metals futures contracts are those within the CME Group, namely the gold and silver Comex contracts and platinum and palladium Nymex contracts. In recent years, there has been a rise in precious metals derivatives trading, for gold in particular, in emerging markets, notably China and India, added to which has been the introduction in 2017 of futures trading on the LME, known as LMEPrecious. To a large extent, this has been assisted by a general increase in interest in precious metals among the general public during the previous bull market.

Another area which accounts for a significant portion of precious metals investment is the OTC market. This includes unallocated metal accounts and a wide range of forward and derivative contracts, commonly offered by banks active in precious metals. These also offer allocated metals accounts.

The advantages of OTC compared with futures trading include the possibility of lower costs compared to trading on commodity exchanges. There is also a higher level of flexibility, as OTC contracts are not standardised (as futures are) and can be made to fit the client's investment strategy. Finally, the limited requirement for reporting positions and activity in OTC products results in a relative opacity, which is desirable to certain investors. However, these advantages come at the cost of a higher entry level, resulting in the market being dominated by institutional and high-net-worth investors. Moreover, acquiring positions in the OTC market by definition means that there is an exposure to counterparty risk.

OFFICIAL BULLION COINS: INVESTING IN TRUST

Bullion coins are widely recognised as a safe-haven investment and a long-term store of value. Although a number of factors play into this perception, what lies at its core is the quality and integrity of the bullion coin itself and the mint that issued it.

As well as unquestioned guarantees over the weight and purity of individual coins, world-class national mints, such as those featured in this book pay special attention to a number of other factors, which support trust in both the product and its origin. These include the ethics of precious metals sourcing, measures to combat financial crimes such as money laundering and the development of sophisticated manufacturing technologies to prevent forgery.

In terms of how the precious metals contained in bullion coins are sourced, this will generally adhere to the London Bullion Market's (LBMA) Responsible Sourcing Guidance, which is designed to "combat systematic or widespread abuses of human rights, to avoid contributing to conflict, to comply with high standards of anti-money laundering and combat terrorist financing practice". In this context, The Perth Mint sources mainly locally mined gold, which then feeds into an integrated process, from refining to manufacturing blanks to minting the bullion coins.

In South Africa, the Rand Refinery (owned by South African mines) refines gold from doré before making coin blanks, which are then delivered to the South African Mint for minting and issuing as Krugerrands. As part of the Rand Refinery's sourcing strategy (and within the remit of the LBMA guidance), the company undertakes annual mine site visits, which provides for a transparent sourcing programme.

Meanwhile, the Royal Canadian Mint incorporates the LBMA's guidance into its own Responsible Precious Metals Program for sourcing precious metals for their Maple Leaf products. Its program also enshrines the requirements of Canada's Proceeds of Crime (Money Laundering) Terrorist Financing Act and related best practices. This best practice is also enshrined in Canada's Proceeds of Crime (Money Laundering) Terrorist Financing Act.

In Austria, the Mint sources precious metals for the Vienna Philharmonic that meet several criteria. First, it must conform to the LBMA and Organisation for Economic Co-operation and Development (OECD) chain of custody guidelines. The Austrian Mint also works under the auspices of the Responsible Jewellery Council's Code of Practice. In addition, the Mint places a special emphasis on meeting environmental standards, which forbids the use of mercury in mining.

Turning to China Gold Coin Inc. (CGCI), which is supervised by the People's Bank of China, the company is mandated to buy all gold and silver from the Shanghai Gold Exchange (SGE). In turn, the SGE only accepts refined metal from operations that are accredited with the Exchange. This guarantees the purity of the gold and silver bullion acquired by the CGCI. The US also only accepts metal, that is used to make its American Eagle coin blanks, that meets certain criteria. This includes ensuring that the gold and silver is US-mined, that it is refined by dual LBMA and Comex accredited refineries and that the metal is ASTM International (previously the American Society for Testing and Materials; the US standards agency) compliant.

Moving to the production process, several mints produce their own gold blanks including The Austrian Mint, The Royal Canadian Mint, The Rand Refinery and The Perth Mint.

Product quality, security and counterfeit prevention are important issues. In the UK, a long-standing tradition, known as the Trial of the Pyx, is a fundamental part of guaranteeing the quality of bullion coins struck by The Royal Mint. Held every year since the twelfth century, the annual Trial involves assayers checking a random coin sample to verify the diameter, chemical composition and weight. In China, once production of the Panda is complete the CGCI will send the master die to the Currency, Gold and Silver Bureau at the People's Bank of China, where it will be sealed in a secure location. In Canada, every die used to produce gold Maple Leaf bullion coins dated from 2014 and silver Maple Leaf bullion coins dated from 2015 is micro-engraved with an anti-counterfeiting security mark. The mint's digital non-destructive activation technology captures images encrypted with a string of code and stores these in the Mint's secure database.

Trust is an essential aspect of bullion coin investment. Trust in the quality and integrity of the coin and trust in the mint that issued it.

Hand engraving tools for bullion coins.

THE
PERTH MINT
AUSTRALIA

THE PERTH MINT

INTRODUCTION

The Perth Mint was established in 1899 in response to one of the greatest gold rushes in the world, which began in Western Australia in 1893. Its fundamental role was to refine gold from the newly discovered goldfields and turn it into bars and sovereigns for use in Australia and throughout the British Empire.

Today, The Perth Mint has evolved into a global leader in precious metals, creating demand for Australian gold in markets throughout the world. Investors and collectors alike trust The Perth Mint to produce the highest purity gold and silver bullion and to create some of the finest coins and bars ever minted. It offers precious metal storage and a range of investment solutions to customers in more than 130 countries.

As a vertically integrated precious metals business The Perth Mint applies the highest standards of quality control throughout the value chain: from refining newly mined doré to manufacturing exquisite coins and bars, to storing and trading metal on behalf of its investors.

The Perth Mint is the only Australian refiner accredited for both gold and silver by the London Bullion Market Association (LBMA). As a certified refiner, weight master and assayer with the LBMA, its customers have confidence in the stated weight, purity and integrity of all Perth Mint products.

It is also one of only a few global precious metal refiners accredited by all five of the world's major gold exchanges: London Bullion Market Association (LBMA), New York Commodity Exchange (COMEX), Dubai Metal and Commodities Centre (DMCC), Shanghai Gold Exchange (SGE) and Tokyo Commodity Exchange (TOCOM). These certifications ensure that Perth Mint branded bars and coins are internationally recognised and tradable, cementing our reputation as a global leader in the precious metals industry.

The Perth Mint's master craftsmen apply more than a century of tradition and expertise to produce an exquisite range of coins and minted bars. Using a unique blend of innovation, state of the art production technology and artistic skill, these

The Duke and Duchess of York visit
The Perth Mint, 1901.

The world record holding one tonne
99.99% pure gold bullion coin.

stunning products are sought after by collectors and investors the world over. From bullion to commemoratives, The Perth Mint creates superb designs with a uniquely Australian flavour.

As a demonstration of the technical, engineering and scientific excellence of the organisation, the Mint produced the world's first, and only, one tonne 99.99% pure gold bullion coin. The coin is the jewel at the heart of the Mint's world class exhibition, where it is destined to inspire the next generation of creative leaders in the precious metal industry.

Among The Perth Mint's most highly desired offerings are its bullion coins, with the Australian Bullion Coin Program being one of the most robust and significant in the world. Each coin is issued as legal tender under the Australian *Currency Act 1965*, a guarantee of its weight and purity. With coins ranging from 1/20 ounce to 10 kilograms, as well as annual design changes and select mintage limits, the Mint offers investors choice and convenience.

In 1987, The Perth Mint inaugurated Australia into the exalted global gold bullion coin market with the introduction of the Australian Nugget gold bullion coin series. Since then, the investor program has expanded to include the Australian Kangaroo Gold, Silver and Platinum Coin Series, the Australian Kookaburra Silver Coin Series, the Australian Koala Silver Coin Series, and the Australian Lunar Gold and Silver Coin Series.

Still operating in its original premises, The Perth Mint is a magnificent reminder of Western Australia's golden beginnings.

The Perth Mint, 2017.

GOLD KANGAROO

OBVERSE

*The obverse features the Ian Rank-Broadley
effigy of Her Majesty Queen Elizabeth II and
the monetary denomination.*

GOLD KANGAROO

REVERSE

*The reverse portrays two kangaroos bounding
across a stylised rural landscape.*

The Australian Bullion Coin Program.

PRODUCTS AND SERVICES

The Perth Mint bullion product range includes gold, silver and platinum coins along with gold and silver bars. Secure precious metal storage is offered through The Perth Mint Depository.

As a certified refiner, weight master and assayer with the LBMA, the stated weight, purity and integrity of all Perth Mint products is guaranteed.

BULLION COINS

The Perth Mint produces and distributes the gold, silver and platinum Kangaroo, the gold and silver Lunar, as well as silver Kookaburra and Koala coins.

Manufactured exclusively by The Perth Mint as the Australian Government's official bullion coin program, the coins are available in an extensive range of weights and sizes. Each coin is issued as legal tender, guaranteeing its weight and purity.

BULLION BARS

The Perth Mint Kangaroo minted gold and silver bullion bars are popular investment alternatives, offering a cost effective way to add precious metal to any portfolio. Displaying distinctive symbols of Australia's heritage, each bar features the majestic swan via the famous Perth Mint stamp along with stylised images of a kangaroo on the reverse.

PERTH MINT DEPOSITORY

Since its launch in 1994, The Perth Mint Depository has offered the only government guaranteed investment and storage program in the world. Located in the safe geopolitical environment of Western Australia and operating the most extensive network of central bank grade vaults in the southern hemisphere, it is a true safe haven for precious metal storage.

DEPOSITORY ONLINE

Depository Online enables the purchase of physical gold, silver and platinum based on value as well as weight. This means owning precious metal has never been easier or more accessible. The mobile friendly portal provides access to live pricing so investors may trade 24 hours a day, 7 days a week and securely store their wealth in The Perth Mint Depository.

LOCATION & CONTACT DETAILS

The Perth Mint
310 Hay Street, East Perth, WA 6004
T: +61 8 9421 7376 or 1300 366 520
   (free within Australia)
F: +61 8 9221 9804
E: info@perthmint.com.au
W: perthmint.com.au

AUSTRALIAN KANGAROO GOLD, SILVER AND PLATINUM BULLION COINS

The kangaroo is the most instantly recognisable wildlife symbol of Australia, providing the inspiration for The Perth Mint's premier bullion coin series. The Australian Kangaroo series comprises four gold bullion coins (1oz, 1/2oz, 1/4oz, 1/10oz), a 1 kilo gold, a 1oz silver and a 1oz platinum bullion coin.

Each design incorporates the inscription AUSTRALIAN KANGAROO, the year date, the coin specifications and The Perth Mint's traditional 'P' mintmark.

Mintages:

- No more than 100,000 1/2oz, 150,000 1/4oz and 200,000 1/10oz gold coins will be produced.
- Mintages of the 1oz and 1 kilo gold coins, the 1oz silver and the 1oz platinum coin are unlimited.

Mintages:

- No mintage limit applies to the 1 kilo, 10oz, 2oz, 1/2oz, 1/4oz, 1/10oz and 1/20oz gold coins.
- Only 30,000 1oz gold coins will be produced.
- No mintage limit applies to the 1 kilo, 10oz, 5oz, 2oz and 1/2oz silver coins.
- Only 300,000 1oz silver coins will be produced.
- A maximum of 100 10 kilo silver coins will be produced on a mint to order basis.

Australian Lunar Coin Series II
Year of the Dog, 2018

OTHER BULLION COINS

AUSTRALIAN LUNAR SERIES II YEAR OF THE DOG GOLD AND SILVER BULLION COINS

The Australian Lunar Coin Series II celebrates the Year of the Dog in 2018. The gold coins are available in 1 kilo, 10oz, 2oz, 1oz, 1/2oz, 1/4oz, 1/10oz and 1/20oz. The silver coins are available in 10 kilo, 1 kilo, 10oz, 5oz, 2oz, 1oz and 1/2oz.

Both designs include the Chinese character for 'dog', the inscription 'Year of the Dog' and The Perth Mint's traditional 'P' mintmark.

23

KANGAROO GOLD BULLION COINS

OBVERSE   REVERSE

1 oz

1 oz

1/2 oz

1/2 oz

1/4 oz

1/4 oz

1/10 oz

1/10 oz

HISTORICAL DESIGNS

In 1987, The Perth Mint launched Australia's first gold bullion coin program. The Australian Nugget was designed by Dr Stuart Devlin AO CMG, acclaimed coin designer and goldsmith to Her Majesty Queen Elizabeth II, and featured four coins, a 1oz, a 1/2oz, a 1/4oz and a 1/10oz.

At the time, the Australian Nugget was the only gold coin series in the world to feature a different design on the reverse of four coins in one issue. The coin designs celebrated four of Australia's most remarkable nugget discoveries: Welcome Stranger, Hand of Faith, Golden Eagle and Little Hero.

Reverse
1987-1989

| 1 oz | 1/2 oz | 1/4 oz | 1/10 oz |

The overwhelming success of the Nugget gold bullion coins soon motivated the diversification of the investor program to include silver, platinum and palladium issues featuring Australia's other iconic fauna. In order to establish the entire program as distinctively Australian in the international market, a new design theme was proposed for the Nugget.

Reverse
1989-1990

In 1990, Australia's landmark gold bullion coin series was relaunched, featuring the country's most recognisable animal icon – the kangaroo. Like the Nugget, the series' artistry, which has since established the Australian Kangaroo as one of the most popular gold coin programs in the world, was created by Dr Stuart Devlin AO CMG.

The one kilogram Australian Kangaroo gold coin is the showpiece of the Australian Bullion Coin Program. As a tribute to Dr Devlin, this release has featured his classic design of a bounding red kangaroo surrounded by rays of sunlight since 1989. By contrast, the smaller sized gold coins in the series released each year feature an annual design change, strengthening their desirability to collectors and investors the world over.

HISTORICAL DESIGNS

In 1995, The Perth Mint launched the world's first gold bullion coin program to draw inspiration from the Chinese zodiac, the Australian Lunar Gold Coin Series. The series acknowledges the folklore and the strong cultural affinity for gold among many of the peoples of Asia. It remains one of The Perth Mint's most popular programs today.

Based on the appearance of the new moon, the Chinese lunar calendar associates a different animal with each year in the 12-year lunar cycle. The series started with the Year of the Mouse and a new design is released annually.

Reverse
1995-1996

Obverse
1995-1996

Following the incredible success of the gold lunar series, silver bullion coins were added to the program in 1999, beginning with the Year of the Rabbit.

All of The Perth Mint's bullion coins are issued as legal tender under the Australian *Currency Act 1965*. Most of the coins in the program feature new artistry each year and select mintage limits to create the potential for numismatic appreciation.

Today, the Australian Bullion Coin Program continues to showcase Australia's famed fauna and the animals from the ancient Chinese lunar calendar.

- Australian Kangaroo Series - 99.99% pure gold, 99.95% pure platinum and 99.99% pure silver
- Australia Kookaburra Series - 99.99% pure silver
- Australian Koala Series - 99.99% pure silver
- Australian Lunar Series II - 99.99% pure gold and 99.99% pure silver

SILVER KANGAROO

OBVERSE

The obverse features the Ian Rank-Broadley effigy of Her Majesty Queen Elizabeth II and the monetary denomination.

SILVER KANGAROO

REVERSE

*The reverse depicts the classic artistry of the
iconic bounding red kangaroo surrounded by
rays of sunlight.*

AUSTRALIAN KOOKABURRA SILVER BULLION COINS

Synonymous with the Australian bush, the kookaburra is the largest bird of the king fisher species. The Perth Mint issues three silver bullion kookaburra coins, a 1oz, a 10oz and a 1 kilo.

The design incorporates the description AUSTRALIAN KOOKABURRA, the 2018 year date, the coin specifications and The Perth Mint's traditional 'P' mintmark.

Mintages:
- Only 500,000 1oz coins will be produced.
- No mintage limit applies to the 1 kilo and 10oz coins.

Die polishing tools.

AUSTRALIAN KOALA SILVER BULLION COINS

The koala is one of Australia's most popular animals, accounting for the exceptional success of the Australian Koala series. The Perth Mint issues two silver bullion koala coins, a 1oz and a 1 kilo.

The design incorporates the inscription AUSTRALIAN KOALA, the 2018 year date, the coin specifications and The Perth Mint's traditional 'P' mintmark.

Mintages:
- A maximum of 300,000 1oz coins will be released.
- No mintage limit applies to the 1 kilo coin for 12 months, after which time the mintage will be declared.

OTHER SILVER BULLION COINS

Australian Kookaburra
*The silver coins are available in 1oz,
10oz and 1 kilo.*

Australian Koala
*The silver coins are available in 1oz
and 1 kilo.*

Australian Lunar Coin Series II
Year of the Dog, 2018
*The silver coins are available in 10 kilo,
1 kilo, 10oz, 5oz, 2oz, 1oz and 1/2oz.*

PLATINUM KANGAROO

OBVERSE

The obverse features the Ian Rank-Broadley effigy of Her Majesty Queen Elizabeth II and the monetary denomination.

PLATINUM KANGAROO

REVERSE

*The reverse depicts the classic artistry of the
iconic bounding red kangaroo surrounded by
rays of sunlight.*

THE AUSTRIAN MINT

INTRODUCTION

The Austrian Mint has been making coins for over 800 years. As well as striking an impressive range of both investment and collector coins, we produce the Republic of Austria's Euro circulation coins.

The company's renown and prestige among investors are not only due to the perfection of its coins, but also the consistency with which it has applied its philosophy of excellence ever since it was founded in 1194.

In 1989, a change in Austrian law permitted the issue of pure gold coins for investment purposes. This is how the idea came about to design a gold bullion coin that symbolised Austria. Numerous themes for the coin were considered until the vote was eventually given to music, the only language that is truly loved and understood the world over. As music is synonymous with the capital, Vienna, what better way to symbolise music than the world-famous Vienna Philharmonic Orchestra?

The choice was not purely symbolic, however. The Austrian Mint occupies one of the most prestigious locations in the Austrian capital. The majestic building is located a stone's throw from some of the world's most illustrious classical music venues, including the Konzerthaus and the Musikverein, the latter the home of the Vienna Philharmonic Orchestra. The Austrian Mint could easily be mistaken for a temple of classical music itself but, historic though it may be, behind its magnificent, classical façade lies a state-of-the-art coin production plant. Here, centuries of craftsmanship and tradition combine with some of the world's leading coin-making technology, much of it developed and innovated by the Austrian Mint's very own experts.

When it comes to bullion coins, our customers trust us to guarantee several key criteria: unparalleled quality, purity of content, responsible sourcing, fair pricing and brand recognition, all of which enable Vienna Philharmonics to be resold with ease all over the world.

*The Austrian Mint in the late 19th
century, seen from Vienna city centre*

*The flagship retail store at the
Austrian Mint in Vienna*

THE AUSTRIAN MINT

The trust that both domestic and international investors place in the Vienna Philharmonic is recognition of the stability and security that a truly European bullion coin can offer. Produced in the very heart of Europe, in one of the world's most stable economies, by a global player in the international minting industry, which is owned in its entirety by the Austrian National Bank, the Vienna Philharmonic is the one and only European bullion coin and it will continue to be so in the years to come.

To provide a service in keeping with its reputation, the Austrian Mint works with a handpicked distribution network. The company has a duty to maintain its brand at the very highest level in order to guarantee the resale value of the Vienna Philharmonic and has made this requirement a key criterion of its sales strategy.

It goes without saying that the Austrian Mint adheres to the very highest standards in every aspect of its production process. We carefully source our gold exclusively from partners that do not exploit their workforce, that employ adequate means to protect the environment, and do not use revenues to finance illegal or ethically questionable agendas.

The solid reputation of the Vienna Philharmonic among investors, coupled with the sentimental value that Vienna Philharmonics often acquire, make each one a treasured addition to a family's assets. The purchase of a Vienna Philharmonic is not only a matter of a sound investment, it may also be related to a personal milestone – a professional success, marriage or the birth of a child – and offering a Vienna Philharmonic as a gift is a most eloquent expression of love and affection.

The Austrian Mint, 2017

OBVERSE

The obverse of the coin features the famous pipe organ of the Viennese Musikverein, recognised throughout the world as the backdrop to the Vienna Philharmonic Orchestra's New Year concerts. Above the organ, the words "Republik Österreich" form a semi-circle, while the weight and purity of the coin, with the date of issue below, are shown beneath the balustrade of the organ. The face value appears at the bottom edge of the coin.

REVERSE

The reverse of the Vienna Philharmonic bullion coin depicts a harmonious assortment of eight characteristic orchestral instruments: four violins either side of a cello in the foreground and the Viennese horn, the bassoon and the harp behind.

VIENNA PHILHARMONIC
GOLD, SILVER AND PLATINUM
BULLION COINS

The Vienna Philharmonic bullion coin's enduring musical motif, featuring the instruments of the Austrian capital's world-famous orchestra, no doubt contributes its international appeal.

Vienna Philharmonics in 999,9 pure gold are available in five different sizes and face values, making them ideal for all type of investors.

The Vienna Philharmonic has been available in silver for some time in the 1 ounce format and, since 2016, is also available in platinum. Platinum makes an excellent alternative investment to gold and has no cause to shun comparison.

Vienna Philharmonics are available without packaging, in a blister pack or in a fine red case. Special gift-wrapping options are available for all sizes.

All three types of Vienna Philharmonic are legal tender, thus have global acceptability and are easily traded at the daily gold, silver and platinum price wherever major bullion coins are sold.

One way of visualising the success of the Vienna Philharmonic gold coin is to imagine that if all the coins ever sold were piled on top of each other, they would surpass the 8,850 metres of Mount Everest. They would, in fact, form a pillar measuring over 15,000 metres in height.

The Vienna Philharmonic gold bullion coin
The gold coins are available in 1oz, 1/2oz, 1/4oz, 1/10oz and 1/25oz.

LOCATION & CONTACT
DETAILS

Muenze Oesterreich AG – Austrian Mint
Am Heumarkt 1
1030
Vienna
Austria

www.austrian-mint.com

VIENNA PHILHARMONIC GOLD BULLION COINS

OBVERSE

REVERSE

1 oz

1 oz

1/2 oz

1/2 oz

1/4 oz

1/4 oz

1/10 oz

1/10 oz

1/25 oz

1/25 oz

HISTORICAL RE-STRIKES

Struck in accordance with their original dies, long after the year of issue shown on them, Austrian Mint historical re-strikes offer the investor a unique combination of antique appeal and the value of their gold and silver content. They can be easily traded worldwide at a rate close to the daily gold and silver price.

Golden Ducats and Crowns are struck in different sizes and face values, whereas the silver Maria Theresa Taler, one of the most famous and most minted silver coins in the world, is struck in one size only.

HISTORICAL GOLD RE-STRIKES

DUCATS

Originating in medieval Italy, the Ducat was first struck in Austria in the early 16th century. While losing their status as legal tender in 1857, both 1 and 4 Ducat pieces were used as trade coins until 1915, the year shown on these magnificent modern re-strikes.

The obverse of the Ducat depicts the profile of Emperor Franz Joseph I, who ruled the Austro-Hungarian Empire for 68 years.

Engraved on the reverse of the Ducat, "1915" is the year that the economic constraints of the First World War brought to an end, at least temporarily, the minting of gold coins.

CROWNS

Dating back to the currency reform of 1892, the Crown became the first ever gold currency in Austria's history when 10 and 20 Crown coins were issued in place of the Gulden.

The profile of the long-reigning Emperor, Franz Joseph I, under whom Austria saw immense strides forward in many aspects of political, economic and cultural life, appears on the obverse of all three Crowns.

The word "Coronae", meaning "Crowns" in Latin, appears on the reverse. The year 1915 is inscribed on the 20 and 100 Crown coins, which is when those coins ceased to be struck. The 10 Crown coin ceased to be struck in 1912.

GOLD RE-STRIKES

4 Ducats
13.96g, 986 purity

1 Ducat
3.49g, 986 purity

100 Crowns
33.88g, 900 purity

20 Crowns
6.78g, 900 purity

10 Crowns
3.39g, 900 purity

OBVERSE

The famous organ of the Musikverein concert hall in Vienna, which features on the obverse of the Vienna Philharmonic bullion coin, was designed by the architect Theophil Hansen and built by Friedrich Ladegast in 1872. Since then the organ has been renovated and replaced on a number of occasions, most recently in 2011.

SILVER VIENNA PHILHARMONIC

REVERSE

*Designed by Thomas Pesendorfer, the former chief
engraver of the Austrian Mint, the reverse of the
Vienna Philharmonic bullion coin shows a harmonious
collection of orchestral instruments under the words
"Wiener Philharmoniker".*

HISTORICAL SILVER RE-STRIKES

MARIA THERESA TALER

Bearing the portrait of Empress Maria Theresa of Austria, the first Taler was struck in 1741. Although legal tender in Austria until 1858, the coin remains popular in North Africa and the Middle East to this day in its original form.

The obverse of the Maria Theresa Taler shows the Empress Maria Theresa in her later years. The Latin inscription on this side of the coin means, "Maria Theresa, by the grace of God, Empress of the Romans, Queen of Hungary and Bohemia".

The reverse bears the imperial crown flanked by a pair of eagle heads above a shield covered in different coats of arms. The Latin inscription translates as "Archduchess of Austria, Duchess of Burgundy, Countess of Tyrol. 1780".

SILVER RE-STRIKES

Maria Theresa Taler
28.07g

PLATINUM FRACTIONAL BULLION COIN

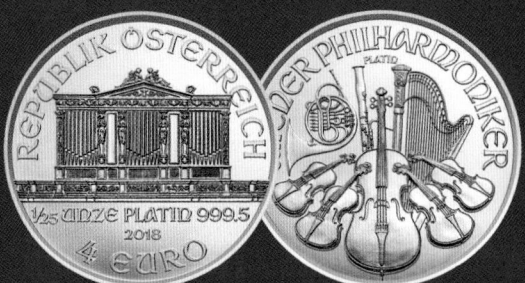

1/25 oz
The Vienna Philharmonic platinum bullion coin
This coin is also available in 1oz

PLATINUM VIENNA PHILHARMONIC

OBVERSE & REVERSE

The weight and purity of the Platinum Vienna
Philharmonic bullion coin appear under the organ of the
Musikverein in Vienna, with the date of issue below them.
The face value of the Platinum coin, which appears at the
bottom edge, is 100 Euro, the same as the 1 ounce gold coin.

Along with the cello, violin and harp, the reverse of the
Vienna Philharmonic bullion coin features the Viennese
horn. Used primarily in Vienna, this instrument employs
a unique form of double-cylinder valve known as a
"pumpenvalve", which was developed in the Austrian
capital in the 1840s.

THE ROYAL
CANADIAN MINT

INTRODUCTION

In 2017, Canada commemorates the 150th anniversary of the Canadian confederation. As the nation celebrates this historic milestone and looks to the future, the Royal Canadian Mint is also looking at its accomplishments since opening in 1908 in Ottawa, Ontario. As a Crown corporation wholly owned by the Government of Canada, the Royal Canadian Mint is a diversified and integrated corporation engaged in four main business sectors: Canadian circulation coinage; foreign circulation coinage; numismatic (collector) coins; and bullion products, refinery services and precious metal storage.

In 1976, demand for circulation coins from a growing Canadian population prompted the need for an additional minting facility. A modern, high-speed plant was opened in Winnipeg, Manitoba, for the exclusive purpose of supplying leading-edge circulation coins to Canada and, to date, to over 75 foreign countries.

Since opening a gold refinery in 1911 to accommodate the refining of gold reserves discovered and mined in various parts of Canada, the Mint launched Canada's first 99.9% pure gold coin, in 1979, distinguished by the stunning likeness of a maple leaf on its reverse. The Mint became the first, in 1982, to refine and strike a 99.99% pure gold bullion coin. Known globally as the "Gold Maple Leaf", this iconic coin will celebrate its 40th birthday in 2019. The "Silver Maple Leaf" turns 30 in 2018. The Mint also refines gold used to produce its gold bars, wafers and fractional gold coins, as well as the gold it uses for its award-winning collector coins. All gold and silver bullion coins are minted at 9999 purity. However, the Mint launched the world's first 5-9s Pure Gold Maple Leaf bullion coin in 2007, which took the form of a record-breaking 100-kilo coin with a 1 million $ denomination. Today, the Mint issues a selection of 99.999% pure gold bullion coins with attractive designs and with the highest denomination ($200 CAD) of any legal tender 1 oz. gold bullion coin.

The diversification of the Mint's bullion offering includes secure, allocated precious metal storage services, as well as the introduction of the Canada Gold and Silver Reserves exchange-traded receipts (ETR), which allow individuals to purchase and trade receipts confirming ownership in physical gold or silver securely stored at the Mint.

Underpinning the Mint's excellence in precious metal refining and its certification as a London Good Delivery refiner for gold and silver is an internationally recognized assay laboratory with analytical capabilities ranking among the world's best.

Refining excellence is also defined by the responsible sourcing of precious metals. To effectively shoulder this responsibility, the Mint has developed a Responsible Precious Metals Program through which it regularly identifies and validates the chain of custody of incoming gold-bearing refining deposits.

As a consummate innovator and industry leader, the Mint is committed to investing in research and development which continues to offer customers the world's best combination of quality, value and security.

The Royal Canadian Mint, in the early 20th century

The Royal Canadian Mint today

PRODUCTS

The Royal Canadian Mint's Gold and Silver Maple Leaf bullion coins are among the world's most popular investment coins with over 29 million and 231 million ounces, respectively, having been sold to date. They are recognized by the distinctive and iconic engraving of a Canadian maple leaf gracing the reverse of the coin.

ADVANCED SECURITY

Focussing on the Maple Leaf bullion coins, the Royal Canadian Mint has created some of the world's most secure bullion coins. The Mint replaced the traditional bullion finish on its full Maple Leaf family of bullion coins, including Platinum and Palladium, with radial lines precisely machined to within microns. The uniqueness of the line width and pitch create a light-diffracting pattern that is specific to each coin. At the heart of the Maple Leaf bullion coin's security features is the micro-engraved security mark of a textured maple leaf applied by laser during the die manufacturing process. This mark gives Gold and Silver Maple Leaf bullion coins a unique "fingerprint-like" signature which can be read using the Mint's proprietary Bullion DNA reader. Within seconds, the security mark is matched to the Mint's secure database, giving investors peace of mind by facilitating the authentication of Royal Canadian Mint bullion coins.

THE VAULT

As part of the Royal Canadian Mint's end-to-end service offering, the Mint also offers secure storage for gold, silver, platinum and palladium bar and coin products. One of the largest precious metal storage service providers in Canada, the Mint maintains a network of exceptionally secure vaults, where it stores precious metals on behalf of individuals, wealth management firms, and institutional investors alike. All metal stored within its facilities is protected by the Mint, a Crown Corporation wholly owned by the AAA credit-rated Government of Canada.

EXCHANGE TRADED RECEIPTS

The Mint also offers exchange traded receipts (ETR) products through its Canadian Gold Reserves and Canadian Silver Reserves programs. ETRs provide investors with a secure, convenient and low cost direct investment in physical gold and silver, stored within the Mint's secure facilities. Backed by the Canadian government, each ETR constitutes a direct unconditional obligation of Her Majesty in right of Canada. ETRs are listed in CAD and USD on the TSX, and receipts can be redeemed on a monthly basis for physical gold and silver in the form of newly casted 99.99% Royal Canadian Mint iconic 1 oz Maple Leaf coins and a variety of bar products.

LOCATION AND CONTACT DETAILS

Royal Canadian Mint
320 Sussex Drive
Ottawa, Ontario
Canada
K1A 0G8

mint.ca/bullion

Stack of Gold Maple Leaf Coins

GOLD MAPLE LEAF

OBVERSE

*The obverse includes the coin's $50 denomination,
its year of issue and the name of Canada's monarch,
Her Majesty Queen Elizabeth II, whose effigy
traditionally adorns all Canadian coins. The current
uncrowned effigy of Her Majesty was created in 2003
by Canadian artist Susanna Blunt.*

REVERSE

The reverse of GML coins is engraved with the following inscriptions: "CANADA", "9999" which denotes the coin's purity, and "FINE GOLD 1OZ OR PUR" for the guaranteed weight in English and French. Radial lines create a light-diffracting pattern. A micro-engraved maple leaf, enabled with Bullion DNA anti-counterfeiting technology, includes at its centre the last two digits of the coin's year of issue.

CANADIAN MAPLE LEAF GOLD BULLION COINS

The Gold Maple Leaf, one of the world's most popular gold coins, was first introduced in 1979. Coveted by investors around the world, the Gold Maple Leaf is known for its striking design and unsurpassed quality—it was the first bullion coin to achieve the superior standard of 99.99% purity.

The Maplegram™ products contains Gold Maple Leaf coins weighing 1 gram in a divisible blister pack wrapped in a sleeve featuring a serial number and assay certificate on purity and weight.

Detail of Gold Maple Leaf

Maplegram25™

THE ROYAL CANADIAN MINT

GOLD MAPLE LEAF

OBVERSE   REVERSE

1 oz

1 oz

1/2 oz

1/2 oz

1/4 oz

1/4 oz

1/10 oz

1/10 oz

1/20 oz

1/20 oz

HISTORICAL DESIGNS

The maple leaf design on the reverse has remained consistent since the launch of the 1 oz coin in 1979 (apart from the purity reference changing from '999' to '9999' in 1982-1983). The reverse of the coins was designed by Walter Ott.

The obverse of coins has changed over the years depicting earlier portraits of Her Majesty Queen Elizabeth II.

Obverse
1979-1989

1 oz

The obverse of coins dated 1979-1989 depicts the Queen's effigy designed by Arnold Machin.

Obverse
1990-2003

1 oz

The obverse of coins dated 1990-2003 depicts the Queen's effigy designed by Dora De Pédery-Hunt.

Obverse
2004-2014

1 oz

The obverse of coins dated 2004-2014 depicts the Queen's effigy designed by Susanna Blunt.

Obverse
2015-Current

1 oz

The addition of radial lines in the field was done in 2015.

OTHER GOLD BULLION COINS

2017 Call of the Wild Series: Elk
Available in 1oz

2016 Call of the Wild Series: Roaring Grizzly
Available in 1oz

2015 Call of the Wild Series: Growling Cougar
Available in 1oz

2014 Call of the Wild Series: Howling Wolf
Available in 1oz

2011 Royal Canadian Mounted Police
Available in 1oz

Vancouver 2010 Olympic Winter Games,
Thunderbird
Available in 1oz

Million Dollar Coin, 100kg

SILVER MAPLE LEAF

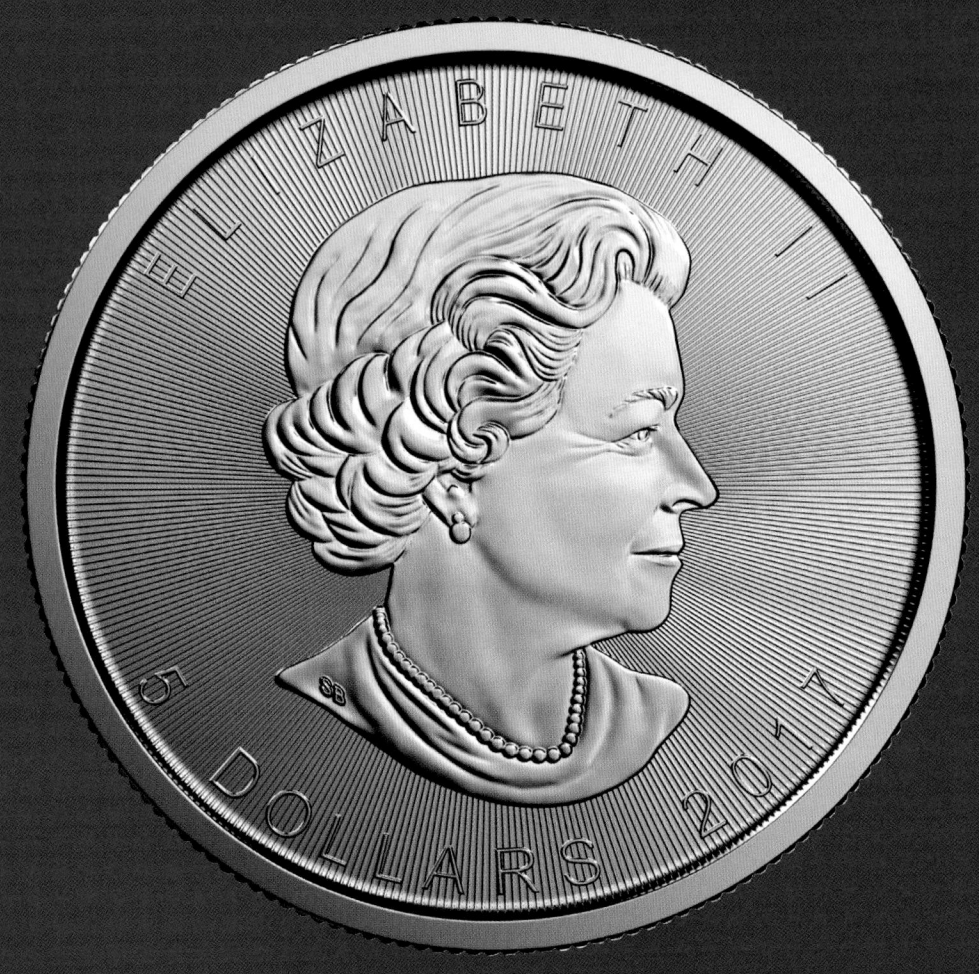

OBVERSE

The obverse includes the coin's $5 denomination, its year of issue and the name of Canada's monarch, Her Majesty Queen Elizabeth II, whose effigy traditionally adorns all Canadian coins. The current uncrowned effigy of Her Majesty was created in 2003 by Canadian artist Susanna Blunt.

SILVER MAPLE LEAF

REVERSE

The reverse is engraved with the following inscriptions: "CANADA", "9999" which denotes the coin's purity, and "FINE SILVER 1 OZ ARGENT PUR" for the guaranteed weight in English and French. Radial lines create a light-diffracting pattern. A micro-engraved maple leaf, enabled with Bullion DNA anti-counterfeiting technology, includes at its centre the last two digits of the coin's year of issue.

CANADIAN MAPLE LEAF
SILVER BULLION COINS

The world's first 99.99% pure silver bullion coin was introduced in 1988. Today, this symbolic maple leaf image stands out from a field of precisely machined radial lines which create a light-diffracting pattern unique to these coins. Next to the coin's central design is an advanced security feature consisting of a micro-engraved maple leaf, engraved with laser technology which, only visible under magnification, includes at its centre the last two digits of its year of issue.

Today's Gold and Silver Maple Leaf coins are Bullion DNA enabled

1oz Silver Maple Leaf coins

OTHER SILVER BULLION COINS

2014 Birds of Prey Series: Bald Eagle
Available in 1oz.

2017 Predator Series: Lynx
Available in 1oz.

2014 Birds of Prey Series: Peregrine Falcon
Available in 1oz.

2016 Predator Series: Cougar
Available in 1oz.

2016 SUPERMAN™ : S-SHIELD
TM/MC & © DC Comics. (s17).
Available in 1oz.

2015 Birds of Prey Series: Great Horned Owl
Available in 1oz.

2013: 25th Anniversary of Silver Maple
Available in 1oz.

Vancouver 2010 Olympic Winter Games,
Thunderbird
Available in 1oz.

PLATINUM MAPLE LEAF

OBVERSE

The obverse includes the coin's $50 denomination, its year of issue and the name of Canada's monarch, Her Majesty Queen Elizabeth II. The current uncrowned effigy of Her Majesty was created in 2003 by Canadian artist Susanna Blunt.

PLATINUM MAPLE LEAF

REVERSE

The reverse is engraved with the following inscriptions: "CANADA", "9995" which denotes the coin's purity, and "FINE PLATINUM 1 OZ PLATINE PUR" for the guaranteed weight in English and French. Radial lines create a light-diffracting pattern. A micro-engraved maple leaf includes at its centre the last two digits of the coin's year of issue.

PALLADIUM MAPLE LEAF

OBVERSE

The obverse includes the coin's $50 denomination, its year of issue and the name of Canada's monarch, Her Majesty Queen Elizabeth II. The current uncrowned effigy of Her Majesty was created in 2003 by Canadian artist Susanna Blunt.

PALLADIUM MAPLE LEAF

REVERSE

The reverse is engraved with the following inscriptions:
"CANADA", "9995" which denotes the coin's purity, and
"FINE PALLADIUM 1 OZ PALLADIUM PUR" for the
guaranteed weight in English and French. Radial lines create a
light-diffracting pattern. A micro-engraved maple leaf includes
at its centre the last two digits of the coin's year of issue.

CHINA GOLD COIN INCORPORATION

CHINA GOLD COIN INC.

INTRODUCTION

The People's Bank of China (PBOC) is the central bank of the People's Republic of China. It is also the issuing authority of precious metal coins that are struck in China. China Gold Coin Incorporation (CGCI) is the exclusive professional company distributing precious metal coins directly affiliated to the People's Bank of China.

Looking first at the production of the Panda a competitive bidding mechanism is implemented to determine the manufacture of the coins. All the mints participating in the competition should produce their sample coins according to the program plan and coin design approved by the People's Bank of China. The mint(s) whose samples are selected by the board of experts shall produce the coins strictly in accordance with relevant technical standards. After the production is completed, the master die shall be sealed by the Currency, Gold and Silver Bureau of the People's Bank of China.

The themes of Chinese precious metal coins fall into ten major categories, namely giant panda with flora and fauna, Chinese zodiac animals, major commemorative events, prominent figures, literature and art, traditional culture, religious culture, Olympics and sports, world heritage sites and places of interest, science & technology and environmental protection. These coins have painted a beautiful historical picture that demonstrates the achievements of China's reform and opening-up initiative, celebrates the time honoured Chinese culture, and highlights the great success in the promotion of Chinese patriotism and socialism. They have also provided the general public with a collection and investment tool, bringing both social and economic benefits to the country.

HISTORY

The PBOC first issued precious metal coins in 1979. Since then, the central bank has launched more than 340 programs consisting of over 2,000 items. Through these programs, more than 7.8 million ounces of gold and 69 million ounces of silver have been sold.

In 1987, the distribution of these coins was strengthened with the launch of China Gold Coin Incorporation (CGCI) which is directly affiliated to the PBOC. As the exclusive distributor of precious metal coins CGCI's responsibilities are twofold. First, it has responsibility for mobilising state-owned assets, in this case gold and silver to produce value-added products. Second, it is tasked with promoting Chinese culture through the various coin issues.

Staying with the CGCI, the company has six subsidiaries: China Great Wall Coins Investments Ltd, China Gold Coin Shenzhen Commercial Center, Beijing Kaiyuan China Gold Coin Trade Center, Shenzhen Guobao Mint, Beijing Gold Coin News Ltd. and Shanghai Gold Coin Investments Co., Ltd.

In terms of its network in China, CGCI now has five branches across the mainland: Beijing Kaiyuan China Gold Coin Trade Center, Beijing Gold Coin News Ltd., China Gold Coin Shenzhen Commercial Center, Shenzhen Guobao Mint and Shanghai Gold Coin Investment Co. Ltd., as well as over 100 franchised dealers across large and medium-sized cities.

*Micro-photo: detail of a chinese gold
panda coin*

The involvement of the CGCI has also meant that the initial distribution of the Panda coins across the country has been bolstered with an international network of dealers, which has grown noticeably over the past 30 years.

The majority of coins are distributed through retailers and international dealers approved by CGCI, while some are sold on commission through commercial banks or directly on www.chngc.net/weben/

Drilling down further, the issue date for each coin is stipulated by the PBOC. Each coin is accompanied with a Certificate of Authenticity (the one exception being Chinese Panda gold and silver bullion coins, though CGCI does now provide a Certificate of Collection for coin sets). Chinese commemorative coins are also solely distributed by CGCI.

According to the Management Regulations concerning the Chinese Yuan in China, the PBOC issues a public announcement specifying the theme, face value, design, metal content, shape, size, mintage, issuing date and issuing background for each coin. The announcement is published by CGCI in the China Gold Coin magazine, www.chngc.net and a number of social media outlets. Commemorative coins with a special significance are announced at the launch itself or in a press release on the issuing date.

Shenzhen Guobao Mint new site

GOLD PANDA

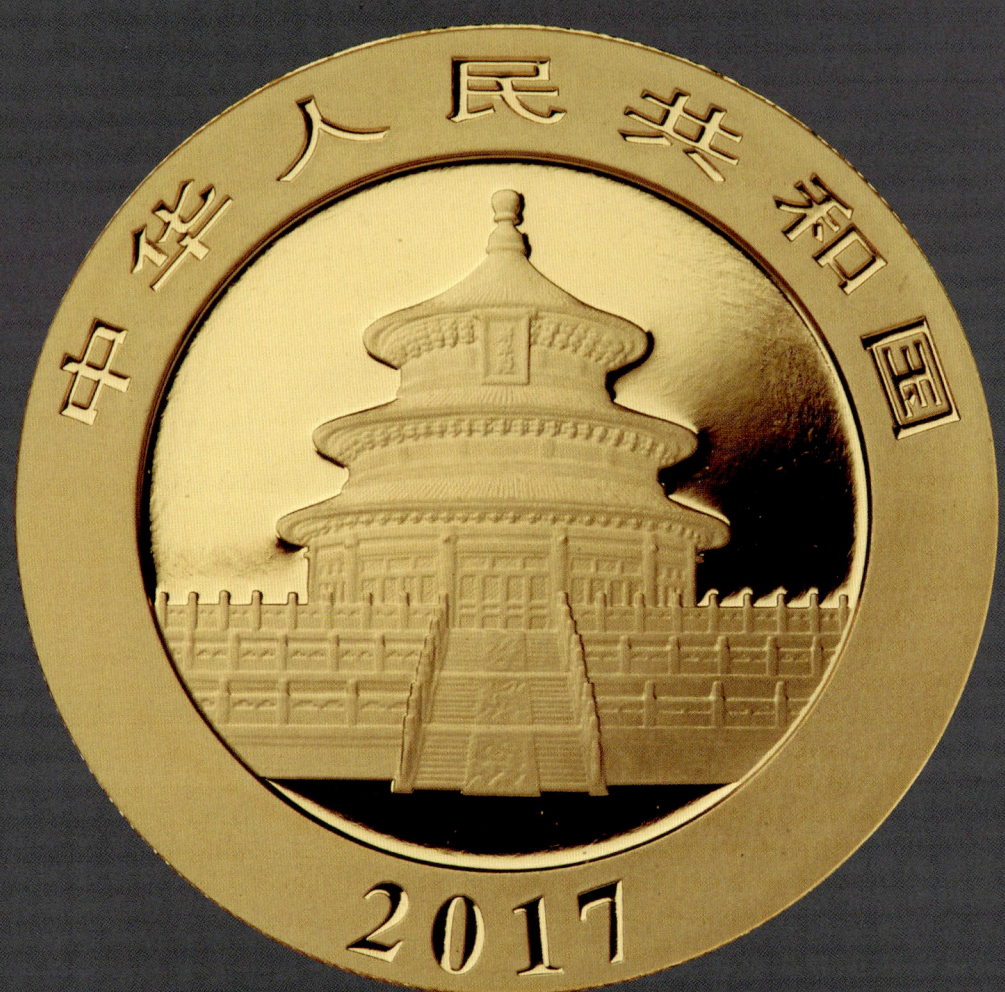

OBVERSE

The obverse depicts the Temple of Heaven in Beijing,
the title of PRC and the year of issue.

GOLD PANDA

REVERSE

The reverse features a giant panda eating a bamboo stalk, the face value, weight and fineness.

GOLD PANDA BULLION COINS

The Chinese Panda bullion gold coin is a legal tender coin of the People's Republic of China, issued by the People's Bank of China. It is minted by the: Shenzhen Guobao Mint, Shanghai Mint Co., Ltd., and Shenyang Mint Co., Ltd., and distributed exclusively by China Gold Coin Incorporation. Chinese Panda Bullion Gold Coins are available in five sizes. The obverse depicts the Temple of Heaven in Beijing, the title of PRC and the year of issue. The reverse features a giant panda eating a bamboo stalk, the face value, weight and fineness. The coin specifications are as follows:

Weight (grams)	30	15	8	3	1
Diameter (mm)	32	27	22	18	10
Fineness (%)	99.9	99.9	99.9	99.9	99.9
Face Value (yuan)	500	200	100	50	10
Maximum Mintage (000 Pcs)	700	600	600	800	1000

Panda bullion coin die

GOLD PANDA

30g

30g

15g

15g

8g

8g

3g

3g

1g

1g

HISTORICAL DESIGNS

Since its introduction in 1982, the design of the Panda gold coin has changed noticeably. For example, the 1982-dated Panda, issued in four weights, did not carry a face value. From 1983 onwards, the gold Panda expanded to include five weights; a face value was also introduced. With respect to silver, in 1989 CGCI launched the 1oz silver Panda bullion coin, followed by a 1/2oz silver in 1993-1998.

In 2016, CGCI changed the coin weights from ounces to grammes. This was due to a statutory law, introduced by the State Administration of Quality Supervision and Inspection and Quarantine, which reflected the preference among Chinese consumers for metric denominations. Furthermore, to help expand its market, CGCI developed two more product categories, 50g and 100g gold coins.

Furthermore, the design of the Panda gold and silver bullion coins are changed every year, thereby offering a wide variety of choices for investors and collectors. Importantly, both coins are struck with a purity of .999 gold and .999 silver. All of the Panda gold and silver bullion coins also bear the symbol for 'proof' quality.

HISTORY OF THE 1982 GOLD PANDA

The "father of the panda coin" is Mr. Zhu Chunde, who was responsible for developing the original. However, the coin designer is the celebrated Mr. Chen Jian, based at the Shanghai Mint. Born in 1941 (in Shaoxing city in Zhejiang Province, near Shanghai), Mr. Chen is also a member of the China Numismatics Society, a board member of the Shanghai Numismatics Society and a consultant to the Shanghai Arts & Crafts Association. Mr. Chen's other notable coin designs include: the 30th Anniversary of the Founding of the P.R. China Commemorative Gold Coins; International Children's Year Gold and Silver Commemorative Coins; China Outstanding Historical Figures series; the 11th Asia Games; Yellow River Culture series and the 10th Anniversary of Hope Project.

1982 Gold Panda

CREATING THE PANDA

A key challenge in translating the image of a panda onto the coin was how to reflect the black and white colour of the creature. The solution involved using intaglio for the arms, legs, ears and eyes, which can absorb light to shine in a black shadow. Turning to the body of the panda, to show this in relief sand-blasting was used to reflect only the gold colour.

HISTORICAL DESIGNS

1983 Gold Panda, 1 oz

1989 Silver Panda, 1 oz

1993 Silver Half Panda

2016 Gold Panda, 1 oz

SILVER PANDA

中華人民共和國

2017

OBVERSE

*The obverse depicts the Temple of Heaven in Beijing,
the title of PRC and the year of issue.*

SILVER PANDA

REVERSE

*The reverse features a giant panda eating a bamboo
stalk, the face value, weight and fineness.*

SILVER PANDA BULLION COINS

Chinese Panda bullion silver coins are also legal tender coins in China, issued by the PBOC and struck by the three principal mints. CGCI is also responsible for their sales and distribution. The silver Panda bullion coin is available in one size. The obverse depicts the Temple of Heaven in Beijing, the title of PRC and the year of issue. The reverse features a giant panda eating a bamboo stalk, the face value, weight and fineness. Its specification is as follows:

Weight (grams)	30
Diameter (mm)	40
Fineness (%)	99.9
Face Value (yuan)	10
Maximum Mintage (000 Pcs)	10,000

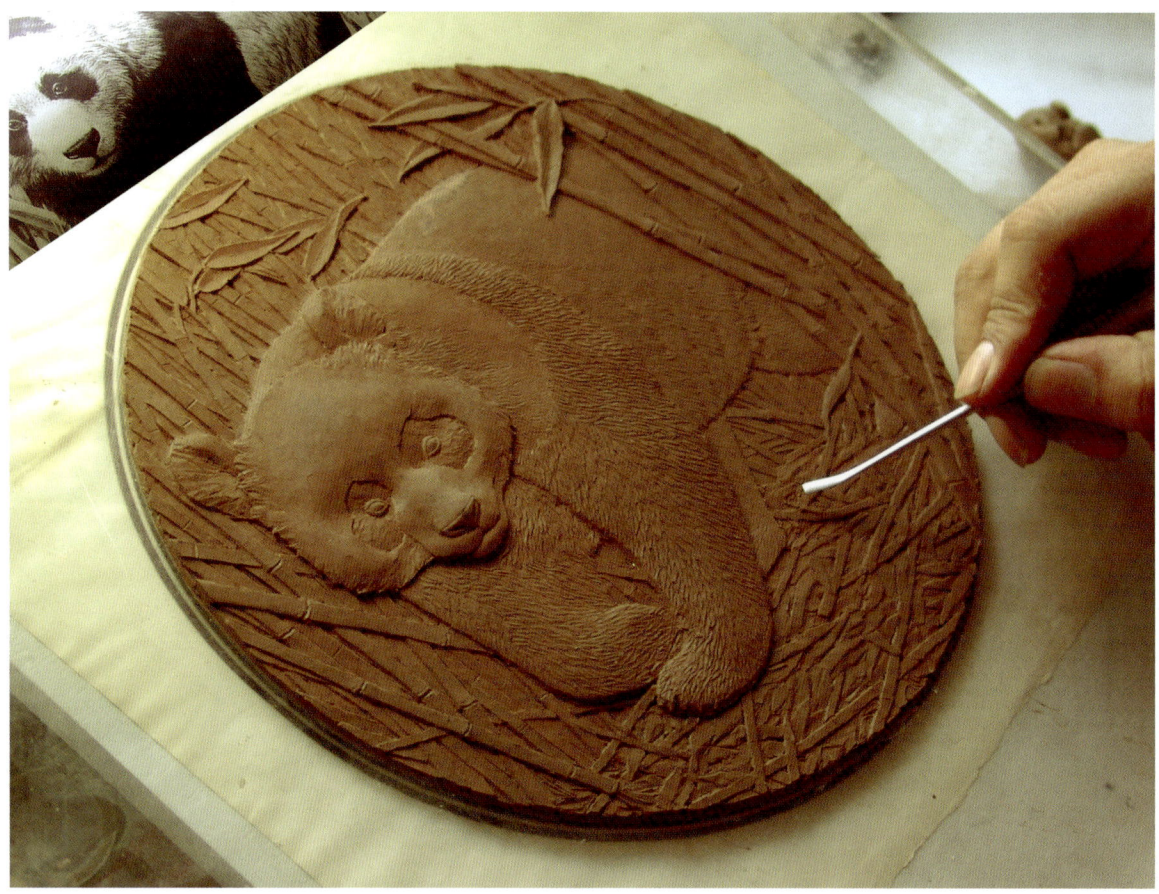

Modelling of clay Panda bullion coin

China Gold Coin Incorporation,
Beijing

THE KRUGERRAND

RAND REFINERY

Founded in 1920, Rand Refinery is one of the leading gold refineries in the world. It is the only London Bullion Market Association ("LBMA") accredited refiner of gold and silver in Africa, and the only LBMA referee refinery in the Southern Hemisphere. Rand Refinery's gold and silver bars are deliverable on the world's leading physical commodity exchanges.

Rand Refinery started its operations at its site in Germiston in 1920 and have refined practically all gold mined in South Africa since then. Rand Refinery also sources gold from other African countries, in compliance with its strict responsible sourcing and know-your-customer requirements. Since 1920, Rand Refinery has refined almost 1/3 of the gold ever produced.

Today, Rand Refinery is owned by South Africa's leading gold mining companies: Anglogold Ashanti Limited, Sibanye Gold Limited, Harmony Gold Mining Company Limited, DRDGOLD Limited and Gold Fields Limited. This means that Rand Refinery is directly integrated into the South African mined gold value chain.

Rand Refinery produces gold and silver cast bars in various sizes, gold minted bars and speciality products for domestic and international jewellery and laboratory applications. In addition, Rand Refinery, in partnership with the South African Mint, produces the bullion Krugerrand, one of the world's iconic physical gold investment products.

SOUTH AFRICAN MINT

The South African Mint started its business in 1892, when the mint produced coins for the Transvaal Republic. The mint was closed by the British Government at the end of the Boer War in 1900, which saw the integration of the Transvaal Republic into the newly formed Union of South Africa.

In 1923, in response to high demand for British coins in the Union of South Africa, the Royal Mint of Pretoria, a branch of the Royal Mint was established. In 1941, the Royal Mint of Pretoria was transferred under the control of the government of the Union of South Africa and it continued to manufacture British circulation coins.

In 1961, when South Africa obtained independence from Britain and became the Republic of South Africa, a new currency, the Rand was introduced and the South African Mint took responsibility for the manufacture of this currency.

The South African Mint manufactures circulation coins for South Africa and for other countries. In addition, they develop, manufacture and market a range of numismatic and collectible coins in precious metals, including the proof Krugerrand.

Rand Refinery and the South African Mint jointly manufacture the gold bullion Krugerrand.

Pouring gold at the Rand Refinery

Punching gold coin blanks at Rand Refinery

THE ROLE OF THE RAND REFINERY & SOUTH AFRICAN MINT IN THE BULLION KRUGERRAND

Since 1967, Rand Refinery and the South African Mint have co-operated in the manufacture of the gold bullion Krugerrand. Rand Refinery supplies the blanks, the South African Mint strikes the coin, before returning it to Rand Refinery for final inspection, packaging and distribution.

In 1998, Rand Refinery took responsibility for worldwide sales and marketing of the bullion Krugerrand, when Rand Refinery took over the business of International Gold Corporation, a subsidiary of the Chamber of Mines previously trusted with the marketing of the Krugerrand.

In 2013, Rand Refinery and the South African Mint formed a joint venture company named "Prestige Bullion" for the management and production of the bullion Krugerrand. Prestige Bullion is 60% owned by the South African Mint and 40% owned by Rand Refinery. In terms of the agreements between the shareholders, Rand Refinery is responsible for sourcing the gold and manufacturing the blanks, the South African Mint is responsible for striking the coins and Rand Refinery is responsible for final packaging and sale. Rand Refinery is also responsible for worldwide marketing of the bullion Krugerrand.

The South African Mint is independently responsible for the proof and collectible Krugerrands, which are not considered to be "bullion".

1967 dye for the 1oz Krugerrand; photo by Clive Hasal, taken from "Krugerrand, Golden Jubilee" by Francois Malan

GOLD KRUGERRAND

OBVERSE

*The design of the Krugerrand is based on the historical
coins of South Africa. The obverse depicts President
Paul Kruger, former President of the Transvaal Republic.
This image was initially used on gold coins produced
by the Transvaal Republic in the late 1800's.*

GOLD KRUGERRAND

REVERSE

The design on the reverse depicts a prancing springbok,
South Africa's national animal and a well-known South
African symbol, originally designed and engraved by
the famous South African sculptor Coert Steynberg.
The prancing springbok was first depicted on the 1947
5 shilling coin which celebrated the visit of the British
royal family to South Africa.

PRODUCTS AND SERVICES

EXCHANGE TRADED FUNDS

In 2015, a domestic bank, Rand Merchant Bank launched an innovative new investment product, being an ETF which is backed by individual Krugerrands. This certificate program is listed on the Johannesburg Stock Exchange. The product allows the buyer to benefit from the liquidity and tradeability of an exchange traded investment product, with the certainty that each certificate is fully backed by uniquely allocated gold.

Rand Merchant Bank also launched a Krugerrand bond, where the buyer of the bond has an option of being paid in Rands or Krugerrands.

In 2017, a large German regional bank will launch a Krugerrand backed ETF specifically for the German speaking market. This investment product will be listed on the Frankfurt Stock Exchange and will be tradeable across all relevant trading platforms. Once again, the certificates will be backed by uniquely allocated gold Krugerrands.

GOLD BARS

Rand Refinery has been producing 400 troy ounce good delivery bars since 1921 when they were first accredited London Good Delivery Status by the London Bullion Market Association (LBMA). The refinery's 100 troy ounce cast bars have also enjoyed good delivery status on the New York Mercantile Exchange (Comex Division) since 1974 and the 1,000 gram bars on the Tokyo Commodity Exchange (Tocom) since 1993. Rand Refinery also produced gold minted bars in sizes ranging from 2g to 100g.

SILVER

In 2017, the South African Mint launched a collectible silver Krugerrand in a unique form named "Premium Uncirculated" or PU, in a limited production run of 1 million ounces. Currently, Rand Refinery and the South African Mint are evaluating the opportunities to issue a silver bullion Krugerrand during 2018.

2017 brilliant uncirculated 1oz silver Krugerrand

LOCATION & CONTACT DETAILS

Rand Refinery
Refinery Road,
Industries West,
Germiston 1400
South Africa

www.randrefinery.com

South African Mint
Old Johannesburg Road
Gateway Centurion
South Africa

www.samint.co.za

Rand Refinery kilobars

Set of 2016 Krugerrand bullion coins

GOLD KRUGERRAND

OBVERSE   REVERSE

1 oz

1 oz

1/2 oz

1/2 oz

1/4 oz

1/4 oz

1/10 oz

1/10 oz

Limited edition 50th anniversary
2017 Krugerrand

50 YEARS

OF THE KRUGERRAND

The Krugerrand is the world's first modern bullion coin, launched on 3rd July 1967.

The coin was the brainchild of the Chamber of Mines in South Africa, who sought to add value to South Africa's gold, and also to make gold available to the "man on the street" in the form of a durable, legal tender gold piece.

The Krugerrand was issued in 22 carat gold, in order to ensure that it was durable and would not become damaged through regular handling and trading.

A decision was taken for the coin to be denominated in ounces of pure gold, rather than in nominal fiat currency. This means that the Krugerrand has a face value in ounces of pure gold.

The bullion Krugerrand benefited from good luck, or good timing, because shortly after its release, the worldwide prohibition on the private ownership of gold was relaxed and then repealed. As a result of these legislative changes, the bullion Krugerrand experienced unexpected demand, because, at that time, there was simply no meaningful alternative product in the world.

Marketing of the bullion Krugerrand was initially carried out by a Chamber of Mines subsidiary named "the International Gold Corporation", "Intergold", which embarked on an extensive (and expensive) marketing campaign. Intergold, at its zenith, had offices in Geneva, New York, Hong Kong, Brussels, Barcelona, Tokyo, Paris, London, Los Angeles, Milan and Munich. In 1976, Intergold launched a global marketing plan, which made the Krugerrand a household name.

Krugerrand sales reached their peak in 1978, when over 6 million ounces were sold.

In 1980, in response to increased demand for gold and a desire to broaden the market for Krugerrands, fractional gold coins in ½, ¼ and 1/10 ounce sizes were issued. This meant that Krugerrand coins were now available at 1/10 the price of the full ounce coin.

In 1985, the United States instituted sanctions against South Africa which had an adverse impact on the demand for Krugerrand. In 1991, the United States repealed its sanctions against South Africa, after the government of the day committed to dismantling its racial policies.

Demand for new Krugerrands did not, however, re-appear overnight, as there was still a significant supply of already minted Krugerrands in vaults in the US and Europe.

The lowest demand for bullion Krugerrands was in fact in 2000, when just over 10,000 ounces of gold bullion Krugerrands were sold.

Demand for gold bullion coins increased in 2008, as the global financial crisis took hold. Demand for new gold bullion Krugerrands was just under 35,000 in 2005, and was 768,000 in 2009. In 2016 sales were approximately 1.1 million ounces.

The Krugerrand went from being one of the least demanded gold bullion coin in 2005, to the most demanded gold coin in 2016. Rand Refinery ascribes this growth in market share to the resilience of the brand, the integrity of the coin and the consistency of the coin through turbulent times.

In 2017, the Krugerrand celebrates 50 years since its first issue.

HISTORICAL DESIGNS

Reverse
1970 1oz Krugerrand

Reverse
1980 1oz Krugerrand

Reverse
1991 1oz Krugerrand

Melting of Sciccel at Rand Refinery

2010 Krugerrand Bullion Coin set

THE ROYAL MINT

CONTINUITY AND CHANGE

The Royal Mint is part of everyday life for millions of people in the United Kingdom and around the world. In the UK, it supplies the coins that make daily transactions possible. As a manufacturer, exporter and employer The Royal Mint makes a contribution to the wealth of the nation, and creates beautifully crafted coins for collectors and investors.

Their influence and products reach far beyond the UK, as they supply coins and blanks to issuing authorities for as many as 60 countries a year. The Royal Mint is the world's leading export mint, trusted internationally for its expertise and the ability to carry out all aspects of coin-manufacture to the highest standards.

Formed over 1,100 years ago, The Royal Mint has survived and thrived by changing with the times. From the first Alfred the Great silver penny struck in the ninth century, to the launch of Royal Mint Gold (RMG®), an innovative FinTech product, The Royal Mint has adapted to the way people live. Since 2010 it has operated as The Royal Mint Limited, a company solely owned by HM Treasury, under an exclusive contract to supply all coinage for the UK.

Today, The Royal Mint is an innovative and modern business based on a 38-acre site in Llantrisant, near Cardiff in Wales. The site is home to coin and medal design expertise, high-tech industrial production, secure storage and an internationally respected museum. It can produce 90 million coins and blanks a week – almost five billion coins a year. The collective efforts of its 900-strong workforce resulted in a turnover of over £500 million in 2016–17.

Bullion has been part of The Royal Mint's story for centuries and is a significant part of its growing business. It opened The Royal Mint Bullion trading platform in 2014, allowing investors a chance to purchase gold bullion coins directly from The Royal Mint. In 2015 Royal Mint Refinery (RMR) branded gold bars were made available for the first time in over half a century. In the same year it launched Signature Gold®, allowing investors the chance to purchase gold from as little as £20 and store it in The Vault.

Bringing its story right up to date and to a new audience, The Royal Mint Experience welcomed its first visitors in 2016. It has been a huge success, attracting nearly 100,000 people in its first year.

The Royal Mint at Tower Hill,
in the late nineteenth century

HISTORY: LONDON TO LLANTRISANT

The Royal Mint is one of the oldest and most respected institutions in the United Kingdom. It has evolved over 1,100 years of history to become a sophisticated design and manufacturing business.

A silver penny struck in the ninth century during the reign of Alfred the Great marks the start of the story. The coin was minted in London as can be seen from the monogram that reads 'LVNDONIA', the Latin word for London. At this time there were many mints, operating more like blacksmiths' shops than factories. Coins were made by hand by moneyers and their essential methods still form the basis of modern minting processes. The Royal Mint has struck the coins of every British monarch ever since.

From 1279, in the reign of Edward I, the London moneyers had been gathered together to form a single mint within the Tower of London. As a royal fortress, the Tower provided a secure location for striking the nation's coins, and gold and silver bullion could be easily delivered by boat or cart. This precious metal was deposited into the area of the Tower still known as Mint Street.

Technical advances, improved standards and administrative changes were made while at the Tower, particularly under the most famous Master of the Mint, Sir Isaac Newton. He introduced measures to improve the accuracy of minting and increase efficiency. With advances in coin-making technology, the cramped conditions at the Tower would become no longer fit for purpose. By the end of the eighteenth century it was clear that in order to expand and develop, The Royal Mint needed to move.

A short distance from the Tower, a new mint was built on Little Tower Hill. It was equipped with the latest steam-powered machinery, arranged in a logical production sequence. Although the site seemed large and spacious to staff and observers at the time, huge increases in demand for coins eventually made even this more substantial minting facility seem cramped; from 24 million coins a year in 1870 to 100 million a year by the end of the nineteenth century.

As the UK Government prepared to introduce a decimal currency, the decision was taken to move The Royal Mint out of London. A new, larger site was needed to cope with the production of the enormous quantities of coins needed for the introduction of a new currency on 15 February 1971, referred to as 'Decimalisation Day'.

The Royal Mint in Llantrisant, South Wales was opened by Her Majesty The Queen in December 1968. After decimalisation, all UK coin production shifted from London to Wales, with the last coin struck at Tower Hill in 1975.

The Royal Mint is recognised as one of the world's leading mints with advanced coining technology and machinery. The latest demonstration of its technical capability is the new 12-sided £1 coin introduced in 2017. Its state-of-the-art security features and composition have led to it being described as the most secure coin in the world, reflecting The Royal Mint's position as a leader in currency security.

The Royal Mint, Llantrisant,
South Wales

A stack of 2017 one ounce bullion Sovereign coins

GOLD PRODUCTS AND SERVICES

The Royal Mint bullion product range includes gold, silver and platinum bullion coins, gold bars, Signature Gold, and support services such as secure storage.

Bullion coins and bars are tested to the most rigorous standards by an independent quality assurance process and their weight, as United Kingdom legal tender, is guaranteed by an Act of Parliament.

COINS

Royal Mint Bullion produces and distributes the gold Sovereign coin, Britannia gold and silver coins, and a highly successful Lunar series. We also produce exclusive designs for global distribution such as The Queen's Beasts Collection.

BARS & ROUNDS

Royal Mint Bullion licenses the right to produce precious metal bars and rounds in different parts of the world. Royal Mint Refinery was launched over 200 years ago and licenced to Nathan Rothschild in 1845, becoming the main global refiner of all gold by 1900. The license agreements allow for bars and other products to be dual-branded.

SIGNATURE GOLD

Signature Gold is a simple and cost-effective way to own physical gold in quantities to suit all budgets, allowing people to purchase and own a fractional amount of large 400oz gold bars that are held securely in The Vault. Unlike buying coins or bars, this allows customersto purchase gold based on value rather than weight. For many, Signature Gold is a practical route to owning gold.

GOLD INVESTMENTS AS PART OF PENSIONS

As of August 2014, the Financial Conduct Authority (FCA) added physical gold bullion to its list of standard assets, allowing physical gold to be included in a pension portfolio. Our Gold for Pensions offer gives individuals and pension scheme providers access to an online account through which they can manage gold held within pension schemes.

THE VAULT

The Vault is The Royal Mint's purpose-built precious metal storage facility located in our 38-acre site near Cardiff, the capital of Wales. The Vault was built to Federal Standard 832 Class A in 1986 and is guarded by trained security staff, on-site 24 hours a day, 7 days a week, 365 days a year.

LOCATION & CONTACT DETAILS

The Royal Mint Limited
Llantrisant,
Pontyclun, CF72 8YT
United Kingdom

Telephone our customer service team:
From the UK: 0345 600 5014
From overseas: +44 1443 235 908
Mon-Thurs: 08:30am to 4:30pm GMT
Fri: 08:30am to 4:00pm GMT

Email our customer services team:
enquiries@royalmintbullion.com

GOLD BRITANNIA

OBVERSE

The portrait of Her Majesty The Queen is by Royal Mint
coin designer Jody Clark.

GOLD BRITANNIA

REVERSE

The design features Philip Nathan's interpretation
of Britannia, first created in 1987.

THE ROYAL MINT

GOLD BRITANNIA

OBVERSE   REVERSE

1 oz

1 oz

1/2 oz

1/2 oz

1/4 oz

1/4 oz

1/10 oz

1/10 oz

A CONSTANT THROUGH CHANGE

The Sovereign has a history that no other coin struck today can match. It was established in 1489 when the first Tudor king, Henry VII demanded a 'new money of gold'. England had a circulating gold coinage for over 100 years before this time but the new coin was to be the largest coin ever seen in the country, both in size and value, and was to be called a Sovereign.

The name fitted the new coin, suggesting a close association with the monarch himself. The obverse featured a portrait of the king and the reverse depicted the Royal Arms. Its purpose was to reinforce the position of the king and to support a political message of stability. It was struck in turn by each of the Tudor monarchs, coming to an end early in the reign of James I, when the crowns of England and Scotland were united. A Sovereign was not to appear again for 200 years.

The 1817 Sovereign with Benedetto Pistrucci's St George on the reverse.

Following the defeat of Napoleon at Waterloo, a great coinage reform was undertaken in Britain and gold was adopted as the 'sole Standard Measure of Value'. A new gold 20-shilling coin was created as the Gold Standard was introduced and given the revived name of Sovereign.

Almost half the weight and diameter of the original Sovereign, the new gold coin of 1817 more than matched its predecessor in the beauty of its design. The traditional heraldic reverse was abandoned in favour of a Greek-inspired St George and the dragon by the Italian engraver Benedetto Pistrucci.

This graceful, dramatic design set the 'modern' Sovereign apart from every gold coin that had gone before. Pistrucci's St George is strongly reminiscent of the marble relief sculptures from the Parthenon in Greece. His design is one of great classical beauty and is widely recognised as a masterpiece of numismatic art.

Pistrucci's design lives on in the twenty-first century and has only been replaced four times during Queen Elizabeth II's reign. It was replaced in 1989 for the commemorative coins celebrating the 500th anniversary of the original Tudor Sovereign, in 2002 for The Queen's Golden Jubilee, again in 2005, and also in 2012 for The Queen's Diamond Jubilee.

Pistrucci's original artwork

In 2017 The Royal Mint marks a defining moment in The Sovereign's history, looking back 200 years to the moment the gold coin was revived and Benedetto Pistrucci created his dynamic masterpiece.

OTHER GOLD BULLION COINS

The Sovereign
7.988g / *916.7*
Also available in 3.99g

The Queen's Beasts
The Griffin of Edward III, 1oz
31.21g / 999.9 / 1 troy oz
Also available in 1/4oz

The Queen's Beasts
The Lion of England, 1oz
31.21g / 999.9 / 1 troy oz
Also available in 1/4oz

Lunar Year of the Rooster, 1oz
31.21g / 999.9 / 1 troy oz
Also available in 1/4oz

OBVERSE

*The portrait of Her Majesty The Queen is by Royal Mint
coin designer Jody Clark.*

REVERSE

*The design features Philip Nathan's interpretation
of Britannia, first created in 1987.*

THE QUEEN'S BEASTS AND LUNAR BULLION COINS

THE QUEEN'S BEASTS

The Queen's Beasts Collection is a series of ten coins from The Royal Mint, inspired by the ancestral beasts of heraldry, myth and legend that have watched over Queen Elizabeth II throughout her unprecedented reign.

The latest addition to our Queen's Beasts bullion range takes its inspiration from centuries of royal heraldry. The background for this range comes from the coronation of Queen Elizabeth II, where ten heraldic beasts stood guard, The Queen's Beasts, sculpted by James Woodford RA for the coronation ceremony.

The Queen's Beasts 2017 The Red Dragon of Wales 1oz bullion stacks

The coins each depict one of The Queen's Beasts, reimagined by Royal Mint coin designer Jody Clark. He also created the most recent definitive coinage portrait of Her Majesty to appear on United Kingdom coins. The Red Dragon of Wales is the third in a series of ten designs that will celebrate each of The Queen's Beasts, including

the Lion of England and the Unicorn of Scotland. The Celtic dragon represents sovereignty and power. The Welsh dragon was used in the Royal Arms in the sixteenth century and the Red Dragon of Cadwallader is the emblem of Wales.

LUNAR

Our Lunar collection is a fusion of British and Chinese traditions and celebrates the Chinese zodiac on gold and silver Bullion coins. In 2014 The Royal Mint struck the United Kingdom's first Lunar coins for the Year of The Horse, beginning a new series, The Shengxiào Collection. The Chinese first arrived in Britain in the early nineteenth century and the British Chinese community is thought to be the oldest Chinese community in Western Europe.

The connection between China and the UK has developed further, with China hosting the 2008 Olympic Games, before handing the baton on to London. A series of cultural and business exchanges and exhibitions have increased awareness about Chinese culture in the UK. The Shēngxiào Collection is a celebration of the United Kingdom's diverse multicultural society, created with the unrivalled experience, heritage and craftsmanship of The Royal Mint.

OTHER SILVER BULLION COINS

The Queen's Beasts
The Lion of England, 2oz
62.42g / 999.9 / 2 troy oz
Also available in 10oz

The Queen's Beasts
The Griffin of Edward III, 2oz
62.42g / 999.9 / 2 troy oz
Also available in 10oz

Lunar Year of the Monkey
31.21g / 999 / 1 troy oz

Lunar Year of the Rooster, 1oz
31.21g / 999 / 1 troy oz

Landmarks of Britain: Big Ben, 1oz
31.21g / 999 / 1 troy oz

PLATINUM QUEEN'S BEASTS

OBVERSE

*The obverse of the coin features the fifth portrait of The Queen
designed by Jody Clark, created in 2015.*

PLATINUM QUEEN'S BEASTS

REVERSE

*The Queen's Beasts are heraldic figures that were displayed at
Queen Elizabeth II's coronation in 1953. The Lion of England
was the first of this series to be struck in platinum by The Royal
Mint and was created by their coin designer Jody Clark.*

UNITED STATES MINT

INTRODUCTION

In colonial times, it was very common to find varieties of currency in use from such countries as Great Britain, Portugal, Spain, France, and Germany. In addition to local currency issued by the colonies, wampum, livestock, and local crops were also used to conduct business and other daily transactions of commerce. This variety caused confusion and slowed the process of trade and economic growth. The critical need for a standard monetary system became an issue of great concern to the framers of the U.S. Constitution.

By 1776, Thomas Jefferson had become the emerging Nation's strongest advocate for a unified system of coinage to lay the foundation for expanded trade and economic growth in the Thirteen American Colonies. He proposed the decimal coinage system that we use today. Over the next 15 years, Jefferson would become a leading advocate for founding a national mint on American soil, both for practical reasons and as a symbolic reminder of the Nation's new sovereignty.

Jefferson's efforts culminated in the passage of the Mint Act of 1792, authored by Treasury Secretary Alexander Hamilton, which also authorized construction of the first Mint in Philadelphia. The legislation placed the U.S. Mint under Jefferson's authority as Secretary of State, and he recommend one of America's most respected scientists, David Rittenhouse, to President Washington as the Mint's first Director.

The Act of April 2, 1792, established a mint at the "seat of Government," regulated coins of the United States, and authorized American coinage to be made of gold, silver, and copper. Gold was to be used for the $10, $5, and $2.50 pieces; silver for the dollar, half dollar, quarter, "disme" (dime), and "half disme" (half dime); and copper for the cent and half-cent. The Act also provided for each coin to have ". . . an impression emblematic of liberty, with an inscription of the word Liberty, and the year of the coinage . . . " Gold and silver coins were to include a figure or representation of an eagle and the words "UNITED STATES OF AMERICA" on the reverse, while the denomination was to be noted on the copper coins ("cent" or "half cent").

THE UNITED STATES MINT

The cornerstone for the first Mint building was laid on July 31, 1792, at 7th and Arch Streets in Philadelphia, and construction was completed that fall. It was the first Federal building erected by the United States Government under the Constitution. Philadelphian David Rittenhouse served as the Mint's first director from April 1792 to June 1795. It was under his leadership that the Mint produced its first circulating coins - 11,178 copper cents, which were delivered in March 1793. Soon after, the Mint began issuing gold and silver coins as well. While surviving Mint records do not specifically record the event, several sources state that President Washington, who lived only a few blocks from the Mint, is believed to have donated some of his own silver for the coins.

In 1799, the Mint became an independent agency reporting directly to the President. In 1873, the Mint's administrative headquarters was moved from Philadelphia to Washington, DC, and it was established as the Bureau of the Mint under the Department of the Treasury. In 1984, the name was changed by secretarial order to the United States Mint. Since the establishment of the first Mint in Philadelphia in 1792, additional facilities have been established in San Francisco, California; Denver, Colorado; Dahlonega, Georgia; Charlotte, North Carolina; New Orleans, Louisiana; Carson City, Nevada; West Point, New York; Fort Knox, Kentucky; and Washington, DC.

Assay offices were established at St. Louis, Missouri; Helena, Montana; Salt Lake City, Utah; Deadwood, South Dakota; Boise, Idaho; Seattle, Washington; and New York, New York. Of all these sites, the Washington headquarters and the facilities in Philadelphia, San Francisco, Denver, West Point, and Fort Knox remain.

MISSION AND MODERN-DAY OPERATIONS

The primary mission of the U.S. Mint is to produce an adequate volume of circulating coinage for the Nation to conduct its trade and commerce. Its other major responsibilities include:

- Distributing U.S. coins to the Federal Reserve banks and branches
- Maintaining physical custody of U.S. gold and silver assets, which includes moving and storing these precious metals for authorized purposes
- Producing proof and uncirculated coins, commemorative coins, and medals for sale to the general public
- Manufacturing and selling platinum, gold, and silver bullion coins
- Receiving, redeeming, and processing mutilated coins

More than 1,600 employees work at six United States Mint facilities:

- Washington, DC – Headquarters
- Philadelphia, PA – Production Facility
- Denver, CO – Production Facility
- San Francisco, CA – Production Facility
- West Point, NY – Production Facility
- Fort Knox, KY – Bullion Depository

OBVERSE

*The obverse design features Augustus Saint–Gaudens'
full–length figure of Liberty with flowing hair, holding a
torch in her right hand and an olive branch in her left.*

REVERSE

The reverse design, by sculptor Miley Busiek, features a male eagle carrying an olive branch flying above a nest containing a female eagle and eaglets.

AMERICAN EAGLE GOLD, SILVER AND PLATINUM BULLION COINS

In 1986, Liberty, as depicted by Augustus Saint-Gaudens, was selected as the design that would grace the obverse of the American Eagle Gold Coins. The Saint-Gaudens design first appeared on the United States' $20, or double-eagle, gold piece in 1907, where it remained until 1933.

Like their gold counterparts, American Eagle Silver Coins have been produced and sold in both proof and bullion finishes since 1986. They have always featured a rendition of sculptor Adolph A. Weinman's magnificent Walking Liberty design, originally prepared and executed for the half-dollar coin in 1916.

Authorized by the United States Congress, American Eagle Bullion coins provide investors with a convenient and cost effective way to add a small amount of physical platinum, gold, or silver to their investment portfolios. The American Eagle Bullion program was launched in 1986 with the sale of gold and silver bullion coins. Platinum was added to the American Eagle Bullion family in 1997.

What truly sets American Eagles apart is that they are the only bullion coins whose weight, content and purity are guaranteed by the United States Government. Investors can buy them with confidence, knowing the coins contain their stated amount of gold, silver, or platinum. In addition, long-term savers can include American Eagles in their Individual Retirement Accounts (IRAs).

American Eagle Gold Bullion Coins are available in four denominations: one ounce, one-half ounce, one-quarter ounce, and one-tenth ounce while the American Eagle Silver and Platinum Bullions Coins are only available in the one ounce size.

AMERICAN BUFFALO GOLD BULLION COIN

Authorized by Congress in 2005, and first minted in 2006, American Buffalo Gold Bullion coins are the first 24-karat gold coins ever struck by the United States Mint. Containing one ounce of .9999 gold, these illustrious coins are among the world's purest gold coins in terms of fineness of the metal they contain.

With a nominal face value of $50, American Buffalo Gold Coins are available to members of the public seeking a simple and tangible way to own and invest in 24-karat gold in the form of legal tender coins whose content and purity is guaranteed by the United States government.

The American Buffalo Gold Coin's obverse and reverse designs feature images by noted American sculptor James Earle Fraser, once a student of Augustus Saint-Gaudens, for America's five-cent coin. That popular coin, known as the "Indian Head," or "Buffalo Nickel," was introduced in 1913 and showcases the native beauty of the American West.

American Buffalo Gold Bullion Coins are available in the one ounce size only.

1 oz gold Buffalo bullion coin

AMERICAN EAGLE GOLD BULLION COINS

OBVERSE   REVERSE

1 oz

1 oz

1/2 oz

1/2 oz

1/4 oz

1/4 oz

1/10 oz

1/10 oz

THE UNITED STATES MINT

PRODUCTS AND SERVICES

The United States Mint is the sole manufacturer of legal tender coinage for the United States. It is responsible for producing circulating coinage for the Nation to conduct its trade and commerce.

The United States Mint also produces coin-related products, including proof, uncirculated, and commemorative coins; Congressional Gold Medals; and silver, gold and platinum bullion coins.

The Mint's programs are self-sustaining and operate at no cost to the taxpayer.

PROOF COINS

The United States Mint also produces proof versions of American Eagle and American Buffalo Bullion Coins for collectors. The term "proof" refers to a specialized minting process that begins by manually feeding burnished coin blanks into presses fitted with special dies. Each coin is struck multiple times so the softly frosted and highly detailed images seem to float above the field.

An official Certificate of Authenticity accompanies each coin. American Eagle and American Buffalo Bullion Coins sell at a fixed price and can be purchased directly from the United States Mint.

COMMEMORATIVE COINS

United States Congress authorizes commemorative coins that celebrate and honor American people, places, events, and institutions. Although these coins are legal tender, they are not minted for general circulation. Each commemorative coin is produced by the United States Mint in limited quantity and is only available for a limited time.

As well as commemorating important aspects of American history and culture, these coins help raise money for important causes. Part of the price of these coins is a surcharge that goes to organizations and projects that benefit the community.

LOCATION & CONTACT DETAILS

The United States Mint
801 9th Street, N.W.
Washington, DC 20220
United States

www.usmint.gov

SILVER EAGLE

OBVERSE

The obverse design features a rendition of Adolph A. Weinman's full–length figure of Liberty in full stride, enveloped in folds of the flag, with her right hand extended and branches of laurel and oak in her left.

REVERSE

*The reverse design features a heraldic eagle with shield,
an olive branch in the right talon and arrows in the left.*

OBVERSE

The obverse design depicts the "Portrait of Liberty."
Liberty looks to the future in this modern interpretation
of an American icon, the Statue of Liberty.

REVERSE

*The reverse design depicts an eagle soaring
above America.*